The Parish Cantor

Helping Catholics Pray in Song

Revised Edition
G-3626

by Michael Connolly

GIA Publications, Inc.

Revised Edition
Copyright ©1981, 1991 GIA Publications, Inc.
7404 South Mason Avenue
Chicago, IL 60638

ISBN: 0-941050-24-6

Revised and updated
from the first edition,
published in 1981
by Pastoral Arts Associates
of North America

TABLE OF CONTENTS

Introduction 1
1. The Cantor's Role in the Assembly 3
2. The Cantor's Responsibilities 6
3. The Sunday Mass 10
4. Qualifications 18
5. A Cantor's Skills 20
6. Musical Forms and Repertoire 34
7. Helping People Sing 44
8. The Parish Cantor Program 49
9. Conclusion 54
Appendix 1. Instructions for Cantors
   from Official Documents 55
Appendix 2. Resources for Cantors 61
Appendix 3. Outline of Training Exercises 64

INTRODUCTION

Nearly ten years ago I wrote the first edition of this guidebook. I had experimented with the role of the cantor at the request of the pastor who first hired me as a parish music director. He was knowledgeable of liturgy and I was willing, but very inexperienced. Thus began an adventure which continues to this day.

There was little printed material to assist cantors in 1980. There is more now, and I hope that the first edition of this book served to encourage that development. Also, I have grown with experience and continued education. It seems like a good time to share what I have learned.

This book is intended to be a resource to parish cantor programs. It will cover the basic material in a simple, direct fashion. I wish to provide the starting point for those who desire to learn and practice this vital ministry. The information has been gathered over the past years from my own working experience: mistakes as well as successes. I cannot presume to have the answer to every question that may be asked. Each community is different. My goal is to offer practical suggestions, not a lengthy examination of theology, history, or theory.

Instead of using footnotes, I have included a list of resources in Appendix 2. When the title of a book appears in the text, a bibliographical listing appears in the appendix.

Because music programs vary widely, I have tried to find terms that are inclusive. The words *organist/instrumentalist(s)* and *song/hymn* are used interchangeably.

References to the hymnal *Worship* are to the third edition (1986).

In 1980, when the first edition of this book was written, I dedicated it to: *Father Roger G. O'Brien & Father J. Patrick Hurley, S.J. Two people who gave me the right opportunities at the right time.* I continue to be grateful for their support and encouragement when I was a very young, inexperienced liturgical musician.

Ten years later, as I complete this revised edition, I want to thank the communities in which I have served over the past twenty-three years, and from whom I have learned so much:

- St. Edward's Church, Shelton, Washington, Rev. Michael Feeney, OSB, Pastor;
- Campus Christian Ministry, University of Washington, Seattle, Washington, the Dominican Fathers and Sisters;
- St. Joseph's Church, Seattle, Washington, Rev. J. Patrick Hurley, SJ, Pastor;

- Archdiocese of Seattle, Office of Worship, Rev. Roger G. O'Brien, Director, Most Reverend Raymond G. Hunthausen, Archbishop;
- St. Luke the Evangelist Church, Temple City, California, Rev. John J. Birch, Pastor;
- Sacred Heart Church, Bellevue, Washington, Rev. Marlin J. Connole, Pastor; and
- Campus Ministry, University of Portland, Portland, Oregon, Congregation of Holy Cross.

Thanks also to Ed Harris and Robert Batastini of GIA Publications for their support of this project.

A faculty research grant from the University of Portland allowed me the time to complete work on this project. I am indebted to the university for this professional assistance.

I believe very strongly in the contribution that good cantors can make in our musical/liturgical/spiritual lives. May the revised edition of this book assist the continued development of the ministry of cantors and of the spiritual lives of the communities they serve.

M. C.

1. THE CANTOR'S ROLE IN THE ASSEMBLY

MINISTRY TO THE COMMUNITY

Cantors exist because of the liturgical assembly, the People of God who gather in community to worship. The community is made up of many different kinds of people whose lives follow divergent patterns, but they are bonded by a common faith and vision of life which is broad enough to include the variety of humanity created by God. Everyone in this community is called to serve in some way, depending on their innate talents. For some this means serving at worship, or liturgical ministry. For others it will be a different task in the building of the Reign of God. Whatever the role, it is performed because the Church, this community, has a need, and calls its members to fill it.

Cantors exist because the People of God need leaders to provide for the community's worship. Small, informal gatherings, in whatever part of life, can happen spontaneously, for the members of the group know instinctively what to do and they make it happen. Larger events, like school plays, community festivals, family reunions, and parish liturgies require people with particular skills and experience to organize and lead the event. There are specific tasks which must be done to insure success.

Liturgical ministers are called to serve because the Church has a need. We require skilled preachers and readers, people who plan services and decorate the worship space, those who schedule and train ministers, the outgoing people who welcome us at the door and make us comfortable, those who distribute the eucharist during Mass and bring it to the homes of those who cannot attend. And finally, we need musicians, who help us to sing about God, our faith, and our lives.

HEART AND HEAD

In recent years it has been very popular to describe human behavior using the terms "left brain" or "right brain." The left brain is considered to be the analytical, rational, and logical, while the right brain deals with the areas of creativity, emotion, and appreciation of beauty, art, and music. Our Church has gone through a major conversion which can be described using these terms. In religious education we have moved from memorizing catechism books to experiencing a journey in the growth of faith. At Mass it is no longer enough simply to follow every rubric correctly, saying every word and making every gesture at the appointed time. We now evaluate the liturgy by how it nourishes our faith. These are changes from an exaggeratedly "left brain," rational mode to a way that provides more balance between the left and right, the rational/analytical and emotional/creative.

The inclusion of more music for the assembly to sing not only increases their level of participation, it also helps change that balance. The spoken word is usually rational, demanding analytical thinking. Music speaks to the emotional part of human beings, that which is beyond the ability to rationally define. It must be felt.

St. Augustine is quoted as saying that "to sing is to pray twice." That expression is puzzling until one realizes that singing draws on two parts of us. The left brain understands the words and concepts, and the right brain understands and communicates the feelings. To pray in song is to pray from both the heart and the head.

DEFINITION: The ministry of the parish cantor
is to bring the song
of the assembled community to life,
and to assist the people
so that their song may be prayer,
from the heart as well as the head.

The ministerial role of the cantor can be divided into two major areas: **animation** and **proclamation**. From these two major liturgical roles flow the specific responsibilities and tasks of the parish cantor.

Animation

A good cantor helps bring life to sung prayer. Good leadership is very often the difference between activity and passivity. It is the members of the assembly who are the primary music-makers in the liturgy, for it is *their* song of praise and petition. All specialized ministers of music (cantors, choirs, instrumentalists) derive their roles from the primary music ministry of everyone present. Therefore, while the cantor cannot alone make the singing into prayer, the cantor can certainly exercise a variety of skills which will help transform the efforts of everyone present into prayerful song and celebration. It is the crucial responsibility of the cantor to be musically hospitable, to be personally present to the assembly, and to help them feel welcome and able to sing.

Proclamation

The cantor has the unique privilege of bringing life to the songs of Scripture, particularly in proclaiming the responsorial psalm. The psalms are the great songs of the Judeo-Christian tradition. Too often, the psalms are only recited or sung without feeling, understanding, or musical skill. A well-prepared cantor can re-create the power of those ancient sung prayers at Sunday Mass.

Can you imagine a culture twenty-five hundred years from now which has explored our ruins and found only the lyrics of our songs? Those who only read the text of "Happy Birthday to You" would understand little of the spirit of our birthday celebrations. A recitation of any lyric shows this to be true. To re-create the impact of the psalms they must be sung. With good music, well-performed, the psalms can live again as basic songs of our faith.

Because the psalm is an integral part of the Liturgy of the Word, it should be sung from the ambo (lectern), which is the focal point for this part of the Mass.

2. The Cantor's Responsibilities

ANIMATION

The first major ministry of the cantor, the animation of the Christian assembly, can be seen to have three basic responsibilities: leading song, solo singing, and teaching music.

Leading Song

Cantors are important leaders of congregational song who use words, gestures, and their own personal presence to invite and enable participation in song. It is critical to understand that they share that task of leadership with the organist. The organist is the aural leader almost all of the time, setting the tempo, pausing for breaths at the appropriate time, and providing rhythmic energy. Cantors cannot do this with their own voice as well as the organist can, even with a good sound system. Cantors assist when needed, primarily visually. For difficult or new pieces a cantor's eye contact, gesture, and self-confidence encourage the congregation. For other pieces which are very well known, the best way to exhibit leadership is by remaining in place with the assembly, modeling by taking part. If the organist is capable, the cantor need not intrude at these times.

A true sign of leadership is knowing when to help and when to step back and trust people to take part on their own.

People need to see that the cantor's attitude is one of openness and encouragement. Assemblies that sing well have a bond with their cantor. They see the cantor as a member of their group, not a disinterested hireling or authority figure. The assembly needs to have respect for and confidence in the cantor's abilities and not be intimidated.

It's important that cantors always be convinced that *people really do want to sing*. If the cantor is not really convinced, it will show. Isn't it odd that we often need to have someone tell us to do something that we really want to do anyway? For example, it can be uncomfortable to be alone in a large unfamiliar group. We want to get to know people, but it's hard to take the first step. However, if somebody encourages us to turn to a person nearby and introduce ourselves, the ice is suddenly broken, and the process gets much easier.

Singing is much the same. We may want to sing but feel like we might be the only one opening our mouth. The idea of singing all alone in a group is scary to most people, almost as frightening as the prospect of getting up front and singing a solo.

In leading song, cantors can bring us together as that gathered assembly we profess to be. Cantors can help us become comfortable in doing what we wanted to do all along. People *want* to sing at Mass. How many times have you heard from a friend that Mass at the parish across town is so great because everybody sings?

Solo Singing

Solo singing (in addition to the responsorial psalm) is an important way that a cantor can serve the parish. There are many pieces of music that are wonderfully prayerful but which are not designed for the assembly to sing in their entirety. These include pieces with congregational refrains and solo verses and ostinato refrains with verses sung simultaneously (such as many pieces from Taizé). Many verses can be sung by the choir, but others require a soloist. If there is no choir present, the cantor can substitute for them on parts they might normally sing.

Other examples of appropriate solo singing by the cantor, alternating with the assembly, include the penitential rite, antiphonal settings of the Gloria, the general intercessions, and the Lamb of God (when it is sung as a litany to accompany the fraction rite—the breaking of the bread and pouring of wine).

The cantor can also offer pure solo performances, and there are times when this is appropriate and desirable. It can be done before Mass on special occasions, in the time during the preparation of the gifts, after communion, and sometimes during communion.

The examples given above are from the Sunday Mass. There are many other times in parish life in which cantors minister to people as they gather for prayer and sacramental celebrations. Baptisms, weddings, morning and evening prayer, funerals, devotions such as the stations of the cross, and even parish meetings which begin with prayer—all benefit from leadership by cantors. These times need not involve complex music. Even without an accompanist, cantors can bring the unique power of music to these events.

Teaching

Teaching new music and refining music that is somewhat familiar to the assembly are tasks of the cantor. A short practice before Mass is sometimes necessary, although not usually every Sunday. The teaching process is crucial. It is difficult to understand that some people feel that we Catholics, who have inherited over one thousand years of musical passivity, should automatically sing out like our Protestant sisters and brothers. We forget that these Christians in other denominations have over four hundred years of common musical experience. They have an established musical tradition that comes from family life, worship, religious education, and school. Should we expect to sing as well without any systematic parish liturgical music education and with the often-inadequate music education in our parochial schools?

Some people even feel it is an intrusion on people's private prayer to teach a new antiphon, acclamation, or song before Mass. It seems a graver mistake, inhospitable even, to expect people to sing unfamiliar music without some preparation. To omit teaching in this case is to invite failure of the people's singing.

The cantor can and must be a competent teacher of songs of the celebrating assembly.

SINGING THE PSALM

The other major area of musical responsibility for cantors is the proclamation of the responsorial psalm verses and inviting response from the assembly. Good vocal performance is absolutely critical in this role. Clean, understandable diction, meaningful interpretation of the psalm, and sure command of the music are required.

The responsorial psalm should be sung from the ambo (lectern) because it is an integral part of the Liturgy of the Word (see "Instructions for Cantors from Official Documents" in Appendix 1). Because the psalm is different from the other music sung at Mass, the person singing it is given the special name of *psalmist*. In most parishes, the cantor sings the psalm, thereby incorporating the role of the psalmist. It is possible to have two different people serve as psalmist and cantor. In this case the psalmist intones the antiphon and sings the verses while the cantor leads the assembly's response. The verse in the gospel acclamation would also be sung by the psalmist.

Specific skills for the four tasks of leading song, solo singing, teaching songs, and singing the psalm will be discussed in later chapters.

MINISTRY...OR PERFORMANCE?

Cantors are highly visible. A cantor is expected to sing well, doing solos in addition to animating the singing of everyone else. Invariably, therefore, the issue of "ministry versus performance" comes up. Prospective cantors may say, "I don't want to be up there to put on a show." People in the assembly also might declare that they don't come to church for performances.

However, it's too easy for these kinds of questions to become academic. A good cantor is also going to be a good performer. We believe that our priests should understand the dynamics of preaching. We expect our readers to learn and apply the principles of good public reading. We ask our ushers to transform their traditional role and become ministers of parish hospitality and care. Therefore, it is only logical for us to encourage a cantor to become skilled.

Ministry has to be supported by solid performance skills. A poorly trained voice or lack of practice will distract as much as inappropriate "show biz" performance. The skills of ministry and performance need to complement each other, working together for the good of the whole community.

People appreciate a good singer. Consequently, a good cantor is going to attract attention. Performance will distract from effectiveness in ministry only if the cantors are unable to communicate themselves as members-in-common of the Christian assembly who have accepted a special ministry because they have particular talents which they have developed for the common good. A cantor's task is to assist people in praying together in song. A good cantor provides visual and aural leadership but does not dominate. Good cantors will have transparency and a credible kind of humility in their personal styles, qualities which enable and encourage the gifts of other people, allowing those other people to express themselves. A performer gives off a clear message: "Listen to me." A true cantor lets the congregation know that the best compliment they can give is to join in.

When not active in singing, a good cantor will visibly take part in the rest of the liturgical action. This is done for two good reasons: because of personal commitment, and to inspire other people to do likewise. At the very least, the cantor should not distract other people from the liturgical action of the moment. Unnecessary movement and other activities (i.e. arranging music on the stand, reading, overly-visible preparation for the cantor's next part) will surely draw attention away from the appropriate place.

3. THE SUNDAY MASS

Let's walk together through Sunday Mass in the parish. You will be the cantor. For the purpose of illustration, I will mention all options and alternatives. In most situations, every part discussed would not be sung at any one Mass.

BEFORE MASS

The Cantor's Preparation. First of all, you need to arrive well before the scheduled Mass time. You should have already received and studied a basic plan for this Mass. You have already, before arriving at church, looked over the plan and prepared your own role, especially the music. You arrive at the church knowing what is *supposed* to happen, keeping in mind that you might have to be flexible on details.

If you have reviewed the basic plan before you arrived, you are now prepared to deal comfortably with changes and spontaneity. Check in with the other musicians to confirm final plans for this Mass. Be careful to note unusual hymn introductions or interludes, and other details related to the accurate performance of your ministry. For example, do you know when you are supposed to receive communion? Have you double-checked any special signals used between you and the organist, choir director, or other musicians?

Take care to warm up your singing voice. This can be done at home, church, or even en route in the car. Athletes warm up the muscles to prevent injury during strenuous work and singers should do the same. Begin with *stretching* (such as yawning, rolling the neck and shoulders, making a siren-like sound). Then go to *calisthenics* (breathing and vocal exercises). Finally sing, lightly at first, gradually growing in energy. A good warm up is especially crucial if you do not use a microphone as cantor. Most churches are large buildings. To fill them with sound requires great vocal energy. Strained and swollen vocal cords are the musical equivalent of an athlete's sprained ankle or pulled muscle. Good warm-ups and conditioning are the best preventative.

Talk with the priest who is presiding. Make sure he understands any musical matter that may affect his own role and that you understand his plans as well.

It may be necessary to go over some details with an individual reader. Make any necessary arrangements for sharing the ambo. It may be helpful for the reader to remove the Lectionary if you will be using another book for the psalm.

Make adjustments to your chair, the microphone, and your printed music now, well before Mass. I also like to make sure that every liturgical minister has a hymnal. It's very awkward when those in leadership roles cannot participate just because they don't have the music.

Your place is in the front of the room, so that you can be seen and heard easily. This place should be secondary to the ambo, the focal point of the Liturgy of the Word. Whether you use a small lectern, good quality music stand, or simply hold your music, your space and fixtures should not compete with or distract from the ambo. Your chair should be close by to avoid excessive movement which calls attention to itself. However, crossing to the ambo for the psalm should not be considered a distraction.

Prayer. A few minutes before the Mass begins, take your place. Go through the order of worship mentally. This is a good time for personal prayer, which calms the nerves and helps you to focus on ministry, not simply the details of the task at hand. It can easily happen that you get so caught up in logistics that you won't feel like you've prayed during Mass. Quiet prayer helps you to be open to the corporate prayer which you help direct.

Preparation Period for the Assembly. A preparation time of up to about five minutes before the scheduled beginning of Mass may be required. The purpose of this period is the general preparation of the people in addition to any music warm-up that may be needed. It's a time for everyone to prepare just as you did a few minutes before.

If preparation before Mass is needed, you will play a leading role. You may need to teach a new song or review another one that isn't well known. The music portion of the community's preparation should ordinarily be two or three minutes. To use time efficiently, I recommend that no accompaniment be used. Both you and the assembly can hear the singing more readily. Also, brisk rehearsals can often be more easily accomplished without the time delay of an organ which is in a rear loft. Some pieces do require accompaniment to communicate the composer's intentions, but most antiphons and hymns can be rehearsed unaccompanied.

A minimum of spoken words should be the hallmark of cantors, both before and during the liturgy. Speak when necessary, but only then. Do your part to minimize the wordiness that often characterizes our liturgies!

INTRODUCTORY RITE

Opening Hymn. The liturgical function of this song is to unify the congregation, to help them become a better community and therefore a better manifestation of the Body of Christ. Your task is to help accomplish this. You may need to do little more than hold your book high and sing, keeping good eye contact with the assembly, like a good reader. Give simple hand gestures to cue the assembly to stand for the song and procession. A gesture to cue the verses, especially the first, will be helpful. In antiphonal settings, you or the choir could sing the verses, and you would cue the assembly for the refrains. This song is a major liturgical action of the whole assembly. If the song proceeds as planned, the whole community will sing it so well that your own role can be minimal. If your visual leadership isn't needed, either stay in your place and let the organist lead or process in with the rest of the ministers.

Penitential Rite. The penitential rite is sometimes sung by the assembly. In option A (which includes "I confess...") you may be asked to sing *Lord, have mercy*, which everyone then repeats. Option C includes invocations which the cantor can sing ("You were sent to heal the contrite: Lord, have mercy") before everyone responds. In parishes the penitential rite is most commonly sung during Advent and Lent, when the Glory to God is omitted.

Glory to God. Many antiphonal settings of the Gloria are now available. In most cases when this is sung, the congregation will sing a short refrain and the cantor and/or choir will sing the verses. You or the choir will normally intone the antiphon first and you cue the assembly for their response. When the music becomes well-known, little or no cue will be needed.

LITURGY OF THE WORD

Cantors must give their full attention to the Liturgy of the Word. Listen carefully to the readings and homily. This can be especially difficult if you have been at a previous Mass. However, any motion, even wayward glances or looking down to read can easily distract the assembly's focus. Your attention provides strong ministerial leadership by example. Be present to the liturgy.

Responsorial Psalm. Listen carefully to the readings. After the first reading from the Hebrew Scriptures, allow a pause for shared silence and reflection, up to a minute or even two depending on local custom. After the silence, walk calmly to the ambo. This area is reserved as the focus for the Liturgy of the Word, and the psalm should be sung from there (see General Instruction of the Roman Missal, no. 36 and Introduction to the Lectionary for Mass [1981], no. 22). Interpret the psalms with the dignity and drama that they deserve. Good gestures can be helpful in bringing in the people's singing of the antiphon, but they are usually not needed after the second repetition.

The performance sequence commonly used for responsorial psalms is very practical. An instrumentalist plays the antiphon melody first, so that everyone can hear it. Then the cantor sings the antiphon alone. Next everyone else repeats it. Solo verses by the cantor alternate with the assembly's antiphon until the psalm is concluded.

Gospel Acclamation. After the second reading, again allow a pause for quiet reflection. Having waited an appropriate amount of time, a hand gesture by the cantor (or sometimes the priest) cues everyone to rise. If they don't stand before the acclamation begins, much of it is lost. The singing is designed to accompany a procession with the Gospel Book. This is a second book, different from the Lectionary. The deacon or priest goes to where this book has been placed during the opening procession. This can be a special place set aside to honor the Word, or the book can be placed on the altar (General Instruction of the Roman Missal, no. 84).

Instruments will probably play the melody, when you then sing. After the assembly's repetition of the Alleluia (or Lenten text), you sing the verse and lead the final repetition by everyone. For longer processions on festive occasions, two or more verses might be used, alternating with alleluias. Sometimes the gospel acclamation is repeated after the proclamation of the gospel, usually without the verse.

Profession of Faith. The profession of faith is recited after the homily. If your parish can sing it (and sing it well!) they deserve an award, as does the composer. Most parishes recite the Creed, so you have little to worry about. However, if it is sung, at least an antiphon should be sung by everyone. An elaborate choral setting is inappropriate, since the profession of faith belongs to everyone.

General Intercessions. The general intercessions, following the profession of faith, may be very effectively sung by the cantor. A musical setting of this rite can heighten the impact of the text. You sing each intercession and give a cue (i.e. a melodic phrase, eye contact, gesture) for the assembly's response.

THE LITURGY OF THE EUCHARIST

Preparation of the Gifts. Singing by everyone during the preparation of the gifts is *not* the ideal. It is good for people to have a break between the Liturgy of the Word and the Liturgy of the Eucharist. Instrumental music, a choral piece, or a solo by the cantor are more appropriate choices for this transitional time.

The Eucharistic Prayer

The eucharistic prayer is a time of concentration which asks much from cantors. First and foremost, you must be present to the prayer! Your visible attentiveness to the prayer, as a member of the assembly, is important, just as it is during the readings or homily. Even though you need to be ready for each acclamation as it comes, you cannot be preoccupied with preparation.

Preface Dialogue. If the dialogue at the beginning of the preface is sung, you may need to assist in the sung responses until they are familiar. There are two different chant melodies in common usage, as well as other settings, such as the one from Haugen's *Mass of Creation*. Make sure you know which will be sung. Confusion here can lead to a frustrating cacophony which will fade to a mumble. When necessary, rehearse these melodies before Mass, with the priest as well as the assembly.

The eucharistic prayer acclamations (Holy, Memorial Acclamation, and Amen) must be designed so as to flow integrally with the eucharistic prayer itself. They should be changed infrequently, so they can be sung easily and naturally. When this is the case, you need do nothing but stay in your place, facing the priest, who is the focus of attention at this time.

Be sure that you know the acclamation by heart before you sing it with the assembly. Since the introductions will be short (a short phrase or just the pitch), you must be able to catch the pitch quickly.

When you are a new cantor, practice will be necessary to do this. Make sure you know what the introductions will be. Few things can harm a cantor's credibility more than an embarrassed, blank stare at the instrumentalists when the singing should already have started.

If you need to provide leadership for the acclamations, stand throughout the eucharistic prayer in the place from which you lead. It is distracting to stand up from a kneeling position or to walk from your chair. Simply turn to the assembly for the singing of the acclamations and look at the priest at the altar at other times.

The Communion Rite

The Lord's Prayer. The Lord's Prayer comes immediately after the Amen, which concludes the eucharistic prayer. This is the beginning of the communion rite of the Liturgy of the Eucharist. If the Our Father is sung, it should be a setting very familiar and comfortable for the assembly. Musical problems should not distract from this prayer Jesus taught us. When people fumble with notes, it deters their musical prayer. Good ritual music flows out of us as easily as breath. I find that the English version of the Gregorian chant Our Father works very well, and there are other strong settings. Whichever is chosen, it should not be changed often.

When a familiar setting of the Our Father is sung, you need do nothing but sing with the assembly and look toward the priest. Unfamiliar music may require leadership from you, but it should be very discreet and limited to what is absolutely needed.

Lamb of God. The Lamb of God litany has become increasingly important because of our renewed understanding of its purpose. This litany *accompanies* and *highlights* the breaking of the bread and pouring of wine, primary symbols of our eucharist. The music is not important in itself. The focus of the assembly must be on the fraction rite, not on the cantor.

There are various musical options for this. The assembly can sing the three-fold litany in its entirety, or the cantor or choir can sing the invocations ("Lamb of God, you take away the sins of the world"), to which all respond "have mercy on us" or "grant us peace." The familiar three-fold form is not mandatory (General Instruction on the Roman Missal, no. 56). The purpose of the litany is to accompany the rite. If there is a great deal of bread to be broken and wine to be poured, the litany may be extended with extra verses so that it will last until the fraction rite is completed. The musical setting should be interesting but simple. In recent years several have come into common usage, notably the one by David Clark Isele from his *Holy Cross Mass* (*Worship* #339) and the chant version from Mass XVIII (in *Worship* #353 [Latin], #248 [English]). Additional texts, or tropes, are often suggested by composers. The words "Bread of Life" might be substituted for "Lamb of God." These texts, or others chosen by parish musicians, can reflect the liturgical season or readings of the day.

If more than three verses are used it is critical that the last one is clearly noted. Most often the "Lamb of God" text is used for this final time and musical changes (louder, softer, different instrumentation/ registration) can reinforce the cue.

Refer to the chapter on repertoire for musical examples.

Communion Song. Music for the rite of communion should start immediately after the response "Lord, I am not worthy," not when communion procession begins, because there is but one communion, whether by the presider or other members of the assembly. The communion song is a song of the whole assembly, including the priest. Starting at this time emphasizes the communal dimension of the eucharist. You or the choir can also do communion songs, if there is time, but these should be in addition to the whole assembly's song, not in place of it.

The communion song works best if it has a strong antiphon or refrain, with verses which are sung by the cantor or choir. It is awkward for people to carry books or papers in the communion procession, especially when communion in the hand and from the cup have become common practice. If you as cantor sing the verses, be sure to have arranged for communion for yourself.

If there is a song by the assembly after communion, you provide any needed leadership. If none is required, simply take part with the rest of the assembly.

CONCLUDING RITE

Mass ends with the words of dismissal. Any closing song or recessional comes after the celebration is officially finished. However, most often there is a hymn or song. An instrumental recessional or silence (especially during Lent) are options. If there is a hymn, you lead as necessary. Stay in place until the song is completed. The rest of the ministers should remain to sing the entire song, and then you process out with them.

AFTER MASS

The cantor, like every other liturgical minister, is first a member of the assembly. Spend time with people after Mass. Be available and approachable. Reach out to those who seem alone. Your ministry will be strengthened by the personal relationships you develop. After a reasonable amount of time, go ahead with your cleanup duties. It's important and courteous to know what is expected of you regarding details, such as putting away microphones or music stands, and to take care of these tasks faithfully.

4. QUALIFICATIONS

Before undertaking a detailed discussion of the technical skills needed by a good parish cantor, I believe we should identify the most elementary qualifications that a cantor must bring to both the actual ministry and a further learning process. The qualifications are both personal and musical.

PERSONAL QUALIFICATIONS

There is one personal qualification which underscores all others. If cantors are to be what they profess with their actions, they must be open to the Lord in their lives. Without this basic openness to the Lord and a desire for growth in faith, the cantor's role becomes just one more performance opportunity, a charade of ministry. Ideally, a cantor is a member of the parish community and deeply dedicated to the growth of that community. But even an experienced cantor hired from outside the parish community needs to have a genuine interest in the people of that parish and a personal faith that is visible.

Cantors need an innate sense of hospitality. An outgoing smile and personable openness will serve to develop the relationship which grows between a good cantor and the community. When members of the assembly feel truly welcome to sing, and also know that the cantor is a friendly and approachable person in situations outside the liturgy itself, they will be more likely to respond.

Self-confidence and poise allow cantors to be themselves when they minister. Public speaking ability is a vital asset. Reliability is essential. Flexibility and the ability to "think on one's feet" will make it easier to adapt smoothly when mistakes occur or last minute adjustments must be made. The public style of the cantor needs to make the rest of the assembly feel at ease, confident, and attentive.

Finally, prospective cantors must be willing—willing to study, to practice, to deal maturely with constructive criticism, and to prepare well for each celebration.

MUSICAL QUALIFICATIONS

The basic musical requirement for cantors is a pleasant singing voice with which the community can be comfortable. The voice must be strong, but not overpowering, steady and on pitch. A good sense of rhythm and tempo are critical. An ability to learn clear enunciation of texts is also essential. The cantor needs at least a general knowledge of music and basic ability to read musical notation.

Depending on the particular community, this general description might eliminate the operatic soprano or the good-intentioned amateur who loves to sing. The musically sophisticated cantors in some urban parishes would seem pretentious in a small rural parish, just as cantors with modest training will seem out of place in a cathedral. The cultures in these communities are very different. Careful pastoral decisions must be made.

MASSES WITH CHILDREN

The information in this book refers primarily to the Sunday Mass. There are other Masses in the parish, however. One type that deserves particular attention is the Mass with children. Children as well as adults will serve as liturgical ministers at these events which are part of the activities in parish elementary schools or religious education programs. The Directory for Masses with Children (no. 22) encourages the service of young people as cantors. When they are well trained, they can be extremely effective with their peers.

Summary. A good cantor brings to ministry a healthy balance between personal and musical qualifications. An outstanding vocalist with little interest in people could not serve this ministry well. An enthusiastic and much-loved parish member who simply cannot sing or keep a consistent tempo should be directed into a different kind of ministry. Someone who has the skills but is unreliable or unwilling to adequately prepare or practice would not be a good candidate. Someone who has the right "raw material" in both personality and basic voice is worth the time and effort of training.

5. A Cantor's Skills

Prospective cantors who posses the right personal and musical qualities will usually require training in specific skills in order to effectively serve the community. This may be done within the parish, at workshops sponsored by the diocese or other groups, in private tutoring, or through individual study and practice. This chapter presents a survey of the skills cantors must develop.

VOCAL TRAINING

Private instruction in singing may be needed for a cantor to reach full vocal potential. Techniques of breath management and relaxation are a great benefit for all cantors, but especially for amateur singers with untrained but pleasant natural voices. If you need this kind of training, go to an experienced voice teacher.

Elaboration of all of the details of vocal technique is beyond the scope of this book, but it is very important to highlight some major details about diction, that is, the way we shape our words when we sing. Vocal diction is critically important for the cantor, who has the responsibility for intelligibly proclaiming the psalms and other expressions of our faith.

Diction

Good verbal communication between the cantor and the assembly is essential. Singing is a heightened form of speech which can communicate much more than the basic, literal meaning of the words employed. The musical elements can emphasize certain key words and phrases by using higher/lower, louder/softer, or longer/shorter notes. Joy, sorrow, consolation, penitence, assurance, and mystery are intangibles which music can express more clearly and elegantly than words alone. And what words cantors have to sing! The ancient psalms which have been prayed for thousands of years, beautiful hymns of the early Church such as the Gloria, key phrases of the New Testament in the gospel acclamation verse, fine poetry and prose which have been set to music—these are the words cantors sing, and they are worth singing well. These sung texts are part of the assembly's spiritual formation. The music helps make the texts memorable. How often we find ourselves humming an antiphon as we go about our day. As we do, we remember the text and are inspired by it. Liturgical songs are part of the spiritual formation of the community, as are the homily, readings, eucharist, artwork such as stained-glass windows, and liturgical environment.

To be of value, however, the texts must be understood. Just as a homily must be carefully prepared and delivered to have proper impact, the music must be clearly sung by the cantor. Just as flowers and other decorations in the worship space call attention to important places and the rituals which happen there, so too the cantor calls attention to important words and phrases. Also, as ministers of hospitality make sure that all are welcomed and comfortable, the cantor welcomes everyone by making it possible to participate in careful listening.

Singing is heightened speech. It uses the same mechanism. Simply put, the diaphragm puts pressure on the lungs, which provide a controlled stream of air to the larynx. It then vibrates to produce a pitched sound. That neutral, buzzing sound is modified by the throat and mouth to form what we understand as words. The primary physical difference between speech and song is that the vowels are held longer, enabling the listener to perceive the pitch. Because the vowels are magnified, the consonants must also be, so that they remain in proportion to the vowels. This heightening of speech in singing must be handled carefully, in balance and moderation. Extreme emphasis on the consonants, such as heavily rolled *r*'s, seems affected, as if the person is singing into an opera house with three thousand seats instead of a much smaller church. On the other hand, a singer who does not magnify consonants to an appropriate level risks producing a beautiful tone with a text which is virtually unintelligible. **The vocal goal of the cantor is to produce a beautiful sound with a clearly understandable text. Vowels are the basis of the singing tone, and consonants provide the clarity of the text.**

Vowels. The stereotype of the voice teacher who starts each new student with the pure Italian vowels reveals much about the importance of good vowels for a beautiful, sustained sound. For good singing, it is necessary to form *ee*, *ey*, *ah*, *oh*, and *oo* properly. Well-formed vowels, an open throat, and good breath management are the keys to a beautiful vocal tone.

Diphthongs. For amateur singers, the biggest challenge with vowels often comes when two of them are pronounced in succession. This is called a *diphthong* (pronounced *DIF thong*). If you say the word *noun* very slowly you will hear the diphthong: NAHoon. Other examples include *bait* (BEHeet), *I* (AHee), *pray* (PREYee). Notice that a diphthong does not occur every time a word is spelled with two vowels in succession. The words *bought*, *seat*, and *boot* do not contain diphthongs. On the other hand, many words which have diphthongs spell that sound with only one vowel. Examples include *fly* (FLAHee), *cake* (CAYeek), and *type* (TAHeep).

To sing diphthongs in the commonly accepted vocal style, it is necessary to hold out the first of the two vowels until the very end, when the second is added briefly. If the second vowel is allowed to slide in early, the *twang* typical of country music is produced. That's fine for Nashville, but the country vocal style is not commonly used in liturgical music.

A rich treasury of diphthongs is found in the chorus of the old gospel song "How Great Thou Art," (which, by the way, I *do not* use in liturgies!). If the singer flips into the second vowel of the diphthong, an exaggerated twang is the result. Imagine Loretta Lynn or Johnny Cash singing this, emphasizing the syllables in capital letters:

Then sings mahEE soOOL, mahEE seyEEvior God to thee,
HahOO greyEET ThahOO art.
—Stuart H. Kine

Now imagine Beverly Sills or Placido Domingo singing, including almost none of the second vowel:

Then sings MAH(ee) SO(oo)l, MAH(ee) SAY(ee)vior God to thee,
HAH(oo) GREY(ee)t THAH(oo) art.

This opposite extreme is in an inappropriate style for this gospel song.

The ideal vocal style for diphthongs in liturgical music is closer to this second example, but not in an exaggerated way which will draw undue attention to itself. The first vowel should be held until nearly the end, when the final vowel is added. The latter, however, *must be heard* for the word to be understood.

This example is from Psalm (121)122:

I *(AHee)* rejoiced *(reJOHeesed)* when I *(AHee)* heard
    them say *(SEHee):*
Let us go to God's house *(HAHoose)*.

And now *(NAHoo)* our *(AHoor)* feet are standing within your gates *(GEHeets)*, O Jerusalem.

Here is the musical setting of the text, by Joseph Gelineau (from the hymnal *Worship,* #67).

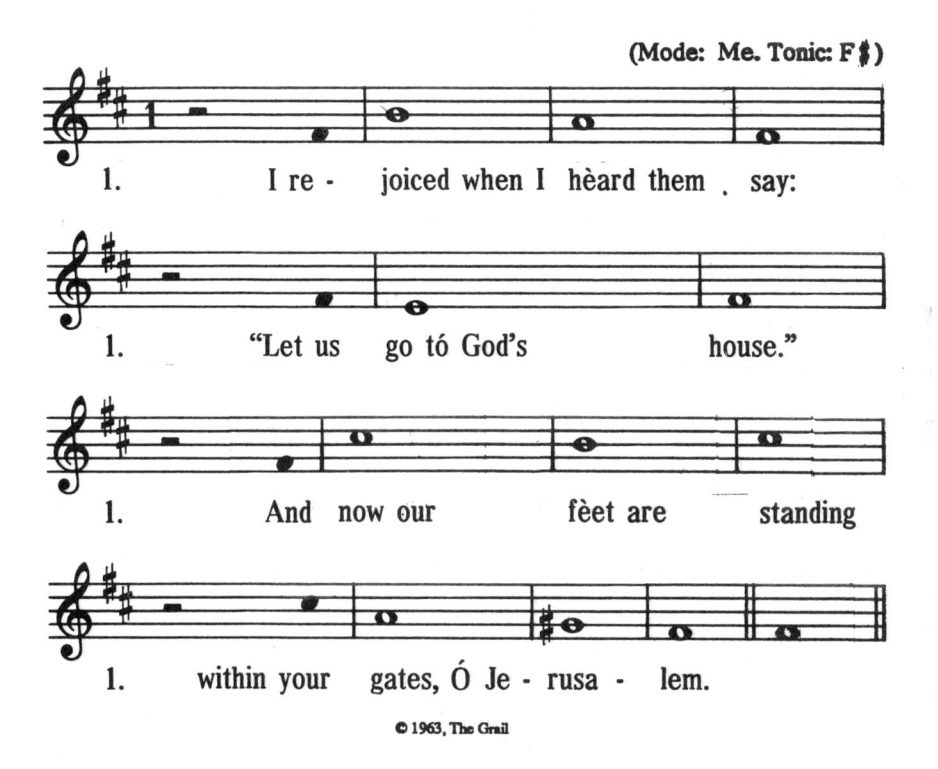

(Mode: Me. Tonic: F♯)

1. I re - joiced when I hèard them . say:

1. "Let us go tó God's house."

1. And now our fèet are standing

1. within your gates, Ó Je - rusa - lem.

© 1963, The Grail

Consonants. Consonants give articulation to the tone produced on the vowels. If they are handled in a sloppy way, the text will be unintelligible. Remember, just as singing magnifies and sustains the vowels, the consonants must be magnified compared to everyday speech.

Consonants are formed in the mouth and throat by the lips, teeth, tongue, and hard and soft palate. Some vowels, such as *d, n, m, l,* and *g*, require that the vocal cords vibrate. These are called *voiced consonants*. Others, like *t, p, ch,* and *sh* are formed without vibration, so they are called *unvoiced consonants*. Carelessness changes *and* to *ant* and *pad* to *bad*. These paired words are shaped identically. The only difference is the voiced or unvoiced consonant.

People in the United States are very casual in everyday speech patterns. Initial consonants are often unclear and final consonants are frequently dropped altogether. Upon careful listening it is obvious that the sentence *I'm going to go to the store* is usually pronounced *um gonna gohduthu store*. The first two words will be pronounced incorrectly and the next three are melded into one. If cantors are to be understood, they must take great care with the text, beyond what they do in everyday speech.

The most frequently overlooked consonants are those at the ends of words. This sentence from the Gloria provides good examples: *You are seated at the right hand of the Father*. The underlined consonants are almost always slighted in speech. It helps to think of this sentence with a different spelling: *You are seateh d'a t'the righ t'ha nd'ah v'the Father*. This looks more complicated than it is. Simply think of the closing consonants as being *elided,* that is, attached to the beginning of the next word. This reminds singers to pronounce each one instead of dropping it.

Identical back-to-back consonants (such as *life force*) are a challenge. Many musicians prefer to pronounce the consonant only once, but it is clearer to do it twice. This is easier for cantors than for choirs. Combining the two can lead to poor understanding. In Vaughan Williams's cantata *Dona nobis pacem,* one movement ends with the words *this soiled world.* If the *s* is not repeated, the text is heard as *this oiled world.*

The most troublesome closing consonants are those which are called *plosive*, because a small burst of air between the lips, tongue, teeth, or some combination is required to produce the sound. In common speech we often delete this small burst by simply stopping the air. When this occurs the word *and* becomes *an*, *Lord* becomes *Lore*, and *God* becomes *Gah*. As you can see, poor diction can approach blasphemy!

While they must be heard, it is important not to overdo consonants. Consonants must be pronounced, but not accentuated by adding *uh* to every consonant (Lord*uh*, God*uh*) as in a parody of operatic style.

The consonant *r* gives constant challenge to singers. People in the United States emphasize this consonant in everyday speech. The reason is that the typical U.S. pronunciation is produced by closing the mouth, especially at the back, making an unpleasant tone. As a result, choir directors often tell singers not to sing the *r*. However, for the text to be understood, that consonant must be present, but in a much smaller quantity and modified so that the mouth is more open.

Careful listening to good recordings can be helpful. In liturgical music, I suggest listening to the recordings of Michael Joncas's *Come to Me* or my own *We Live a Mystery* to hear examples of clear consonants. Popular singers also can provide insights on consonants, even though singing in a different vocal style, because the the pop style emphasizes communicating the meaning of the text. Linda Ronstadt's *What's New* and other albums of jazz standards, Frank Sinatra's recordings of the fifties and sixties, and Barbra Streisand's *Funny Girl*, among others, clearly demonstrate careful handling of consonants. You understand every word!

INTERPRETATION

The technical skills I have discussed are not enough to insure communication of the meaning of the words. Unless that is brought out, the text is just a series of words with little impact. Not all words in a given text are created equal. The important words must be emphasized.

Psalm (15)16 from the Easter Vigil can serve as an example:

O Lord, it is you who are my portion and cup,
it is you yourself who are my prize.
I keep you, Lord, ever in my sight;
Since you are at my right hand, I shall stand firm.

The words in bold give one example of how the text can be brought out. Remember, the consonants underlined must be heard.

O **Lord,** i**t** is **you** who are my **p**ortion a**nd** **c**u**p,**
i**t** is **you yourself** who are my **p**rize.
I **k**ee**p** you, **Lord,** ever in my **sight;**
Since **you** are a**t** my **right hand,** I shall stan**d** **f**irm.

Here is how I set this psalm to music, using this interpretation.

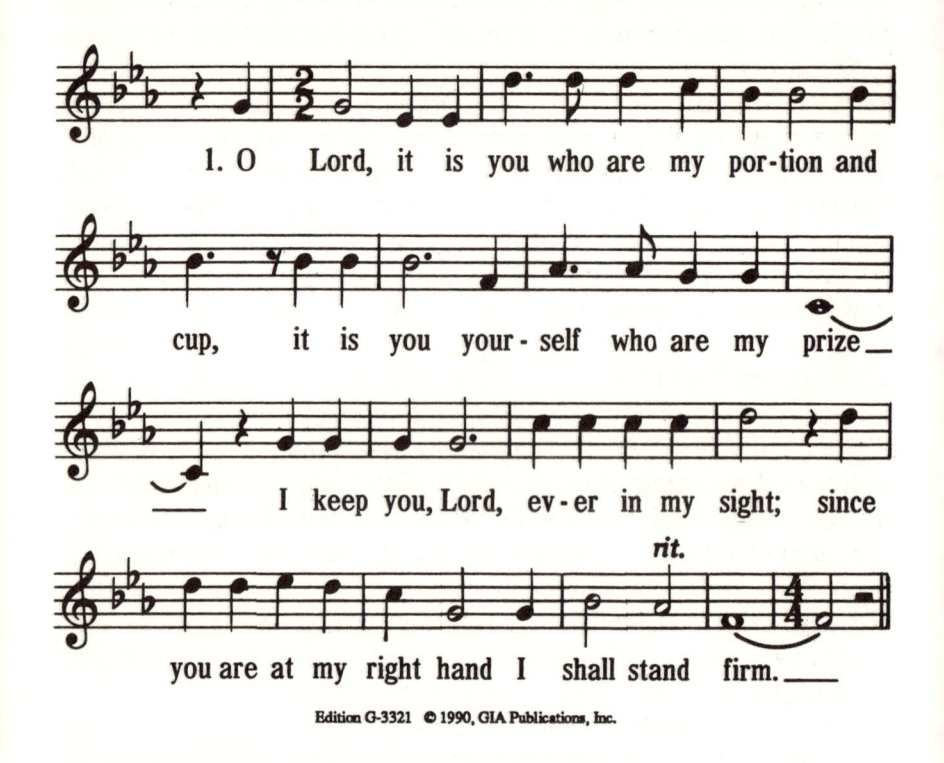

[Musical notation with lyrics:]
1. O Lord, it is you who are my por-tion and cup, it is you your-self who are my prize— I keep you, Lord, ev-er in my sight; since you are at my right hand I shall stand firm.—

rit.

Edition G-3321 © 1990, GIA Publications, Inc.

NON-VERBAL COMMUNICATION

Non-verbal communications can seem forbidding and complex, but this is a necessary area of expertise for cantors. As liturgical ministers our bodies often speak more effectively than words. This can either help or hurt us. Cantors must learn and practice appropriate "body language."

Stance. Cantors must be very aware of how they stand. Comfortably erect posture is the norm. Too much stiffness or excess motion are signs of nervousness or inexperience that the assembly will sense quickly. People, whether they realize it or not, are often uncomfortable with a stiff or nervous leadership style.

Stance involves several elements. The feet should be firm on the floor, slightly apart. Toe-tapping, which is distracting, should be avoided. The knees neither lock tight nor wobble. Stationary hips and appropriate hand and arm gestures are also part of it. Also important is a stable head position which allows movement from side to side (for eye contact with everyone), but minimizes bobbing. In short, cantors must be comfortable in front of people and have good control over their bodies. (The old high school drama training can come in handy!)

Facial Expression. Facial expression is important because it can be seen and interpreted by many people and at great distance. An open, pleasant expression will convey hospitality and genuineness. Whatever the expression, people will be influenced by how cantors feel and express themselves.

Eye Contact. A cantor's eye contact with the assembly assists in developing and maintaining a rapport. If cantors are uncomfortable looking at people's faces, they might start out by looking at empty seats or other objects in the midst of the assembly. There will certainly be some people who would not like cantors looking directly at them, but the assembly as a whole is more comfortable when they feel that the cantor is in eye contact with the group in some way.

An important note: Cantors should not, except occasionally and briefly, look directly at the instrumentalist(s). Cantors who stare at the organist are ignoring the assembly, which works against their effectiveness. Peripheral vision is usually enough for keeping contact with the organist.

Gesture. Hand and arm gestures are basic tools of the cantor. These are probably the clearest ways to signal to the assembly to sing. Stance or eye contact may signal that the time to sing is near, but if the music is unfamiliar it usually takes a direct gesture to bring people in at the precise time they are supposed to start singing.

These initial gestures are, most often, the only gestures cantors need. Traditional conducting gestures are needlessly busy, will not be seen by people looking down into a hymnal, and, except in rare cases where they are helpful, they will probably seem stilted or affected to most people. In responsorial-form music, hand gestures will usually be needed to cue only the first couple of refrains. However, any extended singing without accompaniment or with changes in tempo may require conducting to keep people together.

Suggestions for Gesture. The best principle is probably this: Make a gesture only if it is needed and really helps people. After years of experimentation, I have settled on a general method that works well in most cases. Please bear in mind that it is difficult to fully describe or teach these physical gestures on a printed page. If you need to see good gestures more graphically, go to an experienced cantor or conductor.

A few beats before the singing is to begin, I usually hold out my hand and look at people as if to say, "It's almost time. Be ready." The immediate preparation beat is as important as the downbeat that brings people in. My hand and arm move upward, in tempo, on the beat before the entrance. At the same time, I breathe, and the assembly breathes with me and is ready to sing without consciously realizing it.

I use a hand position which seems to say, "Please, sing with me, won't you?" To form this position, shape your hand as if you are going to shake someone else's (the fingers will be together, comfortably curved, and the thumb separate) and then turn it upward with your arm extended. The gesture universally says, "I reach out to you" or "Come to me." That's precisely the message that I want to convey: "Please, come sing with me."

The downbeat must be in tempo, a continuation of the upbeat. There should be a "click" at the bottom, as with any conducting, to show exactly where the beat is.

After the downbeat, most often I simply hold my hand out to invite continued singing. I might hold it there for an entire antiphon, if it is short, but most often I simply lower it slowly and unobtrusively.

Occasionally gestures will be needed at times other than the downbeat. If the tempo slows dramatically (as during the last refrain of "On Eagle's Wings" [*Gather* #26]) or a note is held or cut off in an unusual way, the assembly will need the assistance of a gesture.

One key to the use of gesture is consistency. My congregations have become accustomed to my opening gestures to bring them in. The trust level builds up so that they depend on the gestures. I know that this is true, because in those times I've inadvertently gestured at the wrong time, people have often begun to sing! Trust lasts only so long if you do that often.

The size of gestures depends on the size of the assembly and building. In small groups, anything larger than a moderate gesture seems foolish and pretentious. In a large crowd, small gestures are completely inadequate.

Another type of conducting can be very handy especially for music which is new to people. The technique has no commonly-used name as far as I know, so for our purposes here let's call it a *Pitch/ Rhythm* technique. It is a style in which pitch levels are denoted by the height of the conducting hand, and the hand travels in rhythm with the notes. I clearly remember an elementary teacher using this technique to lead us in singing. It worked then, and, used in moderation, it can be helpful in church now.

The best use of this technique, as I see it, is in conducting unfamiliar antiphons or other short parts of music which can be learned by rote (see the later section on teaching music). The style becomes tedious if used for long periods of time. When the new music is learned, this style of gesture should be abandoned in favor of an opening gesture or none at all.

In this "Pitch/Rhythm" style, be careful to maintain consistency between the level of your hand and the pitch level. Practice with imaginary staff lines in the air. This will help to establish a strong pitch level/hand level relationship, making the gestures as clear as possible.

For those who lead singing with a guitar or other instrument in their hands, the commonly-used "head conducting" method will serve. Eye contact is even more important in this case, since guitarists cannot easily free a hand. The head follows the same basic conducting pattern as does the hand- smooth upbeat in tempo, smooth downbeat with a "click" at the bottom. It is vital to breathe on the preparatory beat as usual. Be careful to limit the size of the head cue. Too large a gesture, resulting in bobbing of the head, can be comical.

RHYTHM AND TEMPO

The cantor's singing must have strong rhythmic drive and clear tempo. This sense of *energy-in-time* gives the music vital forward motion and makes it exciting to sing, whether the music be a traditional hymn, chant, or contemporary music.

Tempo. Tempo is the speed of the underlying pulse of the music. It is the speed at which the primary beat occurs. In 4/4 time there will be either 4 or 2 of these primary beats per measure; in 3/4, either 3 or 1; and in 6/8, either 6 or 2. Cantors must have a strong inner sense of tempo if they are to lead singing well. If the cantor holds back, waiting to hear the organ, or worse yet, doesn't listen at all, the cantor will inevitably fall behind quickly. **The organ (or other instrument) sets the tempo and the cantor must be with that tempo.**

The spiritual "Somebody's Knockin' at Your Door" (*Worship* #415; *ICEL Resource Collection* #49) is in 2/4 time. There are two strong beats per measure, and I take this piece at a rather brisk tempo (about mm. 108).

Some-bod-y's knock-in' at your door; Some-bod-y's knock-in' at your door; O__ sin-ner, why don't you an-swer? Some-bod-y's knock-in' at your door.__

Solo 1. Knocks like_ Je-sus, *All* Some-bod-y's knock-in' at your door; *Solo* Knocks like_ Je-sus, *All* Some-bod-y's knock-in' at your door. O__ sin-ner, why don't you an-swer? Some-bod-y's knock-in' at your door.__

Sensitive treatment of tempo means that it will not always march along mechanically. Very often *ritardandos* are called for as a verse ends, just before the antiphon returns, and the antiphon begins *a tempo*. The cantor must be in time with the organ. This requires awareness, keen listening, and *practice*.

In large reverberant churches this can be challenging, but it is possible to stay together. If the organ is at the back, at a great distance from the cantor, there will be a time lag. This can be offset by the cantor actually singing ahead of the beat that is heard from the organ. Not only should the cantor not wait to hear the organ, which means the cantor is always late anyway, the cantor must actually sing ahead of the organ sound. In the middle of the church the assembly will hear the sounds together.

Rhythm. Rhythm is the way the major beat is divided to give the piece its particular character. "Somebody's Knockin' at Your Door" uses a rhythmic motive which includes syncopation within the framework of two strong beats per measure. The three bar motive is:

If the cantor does not have a strong sense of rhythm, this energetic piece will sound dull and lifeless.

Once the tempo is clear in the cantor's mind, the key to rhythmic singing is the proper articulation of consonants. Vowels provide the substance of the singing voice and consonants give the articulation and drive. In order to keep exactly in time, cantors must sing vowels on the beat. This means that a consonant which comes before the vowel must be sung *before the beat* in order for it to be heard as in correct tempo. If there is a previous note, a little time must be stolen from it so that the consonant will be ahead of the beat.

Some consonants, like *d, t, p,* and *k,* are short, so they don't require as much time to the borrowed from the previous note. Others, including *w, l, m, n,* and *y* are quite long. If a singer begins the word *water* with the consonant exactly on the beat, it will sound late. The consonant simply takes a long time to sound.

The hymn above provides several examples. The underlined consonants are quite long and must be sung ahead of the beat.

<u>S</u>omebody's <u>kn</u>ockin' at <u>y</u>our door.
O <u>s</u>inner, <u>wh</u>y don't <u>y</u>ou answer?

COMMUNICATION SKILLS

Verbal. Most of the cantor's communication is either musical or non-verbal. Verbal communication is, however, necessary for song announcements and in teaching music. Good public speaking skills are required. Cantors must be clear, sufficiently loud, pleasant and inviting, and concise. When a hymn must be announced, the title and number should be spoken at a measured pace and then repeated. Then, the organist should plan for enough time for the assembly to find the page to sing the beginning of the hymn.

Most spoken communication by cantors is of the practical, "how-to" variety. Comments should be kept to a minimum. Mass is so overloaded with words as it is that cantors should not add many of their own! If non-verbal communication will suffice (i.e. gesturing for the assembly to sit or stand, listing the music numbers on a board), silence by the cantor is preferred.

The Microphone. Most cantors will be using a microphone at times during Mass. They must be heard and understood through the sound system. Practicing with an objective listener can help cantors learn how to avoid "pops," hissing, and other unpleasant amplified sounds. There is a temptation to let the microphone do all the work. This must be avoided. Speech and song produced with proper projection and amplified appropriately will sound more natural than a soft vocal tone that relies totally on electronic amplification.

When they use a microphone, cantors will not use it in the same way at all times. Speech requires a closer distance to the microphone. Singing, which is generally louder by nature, must be done further from it.

There are many different kinds of microphones and amplification systems. Many churches are installing excellent systems which can handle the full frequency (pitch) range of music. It is important for cantors to know what kind of microphone they are using and the direction and distance from which it picks up sound. This varies. Some microphones will pick up at great distance. Others have only a short range from directly in front of the microphone. The angle and distance make a great difference in the volume and fidelity of the sound. This can be determined by practicing with the microphone from all angles and varying distance.

LITURGICAL AWARENESS

Cantors must know the structure of the Order of Mass as well as the function and flow of each part. This basic liturgical education is essential to effective ministry by a parish cantor. A cantor who really understands both the structure and the movement of the parish's Mass can prayerfully and calmly take part in the celebration. If something goes wrong (order changed, prayer is skipped, etc.), the knowledgeable cantor can make quick decisions about how to proceed. To be able to "think on one's feet," a cantor needs to know the order and pace of the Mass inside and out.

Timing and pace are intangible but very important skills for cantors to master. Experience will give cantors a sense of when to speed up or slow down their particular parts in the celebration in a way that blends with other factors, such as the priest's style, the season, or the hour of the day.

PREPARATION

Cantors must know how to prepare for each liturgy. They need to know not only the way the Mass generally flows at the parish, but how it will proceed in this specific instance.

Adequate preparation means that cantors must nearly memorize the order so that only quick, infrequent glances at a list will be needed during Mass. Much of the music will be memorized. The acclamations will be quickly mastered because of their repetition. The psalm and hymns must be carefully rehearsed so that eye contact can be maintained with the assembly.

6. Musical Forms and Repertoire

MUSICAL FORMS

Cantors must be well versed in several distinct musical forms:

Hymns and Songs—pieces that are sung in their entirety by everyone
Acclamations—short, strong pieces integral to the flow of the rite
Responses—short phrases sung in dialog with the presider
Responsorial pieces—in which everyone sings a short antiphon after the cantor and/or choir sings the verses
Litanies—in which the assembly repeats a short refrain after each of several invocations by the cantor

Hymns and Songs

Hymns and songs are quite straightforward. The tempo is set by the instrumentalists who maintain the real aural leadership of the music. A well-designed, balanced organ played properly will lead more effectively than a cantor singing into a microphone. The cantor primarily provides visual leadership and should not, generally, use the microphone at all for hymns.

A fine organist will lead so clearly that little or no rehearsal with the cantor is needed for hymns. Unfortunately, every parish is not blessed with a highly skilled organist, so some rehearsal or clarification of details may be needed. It is important for the cantor to know how the organist will handle the transition from the end of one verse to the beginning of the next. Will there be a ritard? How long will the break be between the final chord and the next verse? A useful norm for this is that the break should be one full beat, in tempo. Is there a written-out interlude between verses, as in "Gather Us In" (*Worship* #665; *Gather* #311)? Will the organist improvise an interlude or modulation? If so, how will that be signaled and what is the cue to sing the next verse? Are there notes in the middle of the hymn which will be held longer than written? This occurs in "All Creatures of Our God and King" (*Worship* #520).

Acclamations

The acclamations include the Gospel Acclamation (Alleluia, except in Lent), Holy, Memorial Acclamation, and Amen. For cantors, they are more complex than hymns and songs. Because the introduction will be short, it is necessary for the cantor to quickly sense the tempo and be with it immediately. Unfamiliar music will require more leadership from the cantor, but as the setting is repeated and becomes well known, fewer or no gestures will be needed and reliance on the microphone will be a hindrance.

In the United States, the most commonly sung acclamations for the eucharistic prayer are from *A Community Mass,* by Richard Proulx (*Worship* #243-244) and *Mass of Creation* by Marty Haugen (*Gather* #77-79).

Most acclamations are composed to be sung in their entirety by the assembly. Others are written so that the cantor or choir sings some parts alone while the assembly sings at other times. The assembly may simply repeat after the cantor or choir, or there may be a repeated refrain. The latter is the case in the Holy and Memorial Acclamation from the *Mass of the Divine Word* by Br. Howard Hughes, SM (*Worship* #311-312).

The second and third eucharistic prayers for children include additional short acclamations. The cantor's leadership here is important since this deviates from the standard format. Two settings of the second prayer are included in the *Hymnal for Catholic Students*—one by Richard Proulx and the other an adaptation of Marty Haugen's *Mass of Creation.*

Responses

At times some parts of the dialog between the priest and the rest of the assembly will be sung. This may be as simple as a sung Amen at the end of a sung prayer or more developed, as in the dialog at the beginning of the preface of the eucharistic prayer (*Worship* #242). The cantor takes part with the rest of the assembly, but active leadership is usually not necessary. If the response is unfamiliar, it should be rehearsed before Mass. Gestures may be helpful until the music is well known, at which time they should be omitted.

Responsorial Music

The responsorial form is used in many psalm settings and contemporary songs. The term *responsorial* refers to the form in which the cantor or choir sings verses interspersed with the assembly's response or refrain. The responsorial psalm of the Mass is given that name because of the musical form, not because it is a response to the first reading, ev though the psalm is usually related to the reading in some way. Another term for the refrain is *antiphon*.

The verses of responsorial pieces are one time that the cantor may set the tempo. In pieces with expressive, free verses, such as psalm tones, the organist will act as an *accompanist* to the cantor rather than the aural leader. At other times, when the music maintains a strong sense of tempo, the cantor still must follow the organist's tempo leadership.

Litanies

Litanies are prayers of petition in which a short phrase, or invocation, is sung by the cantor or spoken by another minister, and all respond with a short phrase. Examples in the Mass include the Penitential Rite, Form C (Cantor: *You were sent to heal the contrite: Lord, have mercy.* All: *Lord have mercy*), the General Intercessions, and Lamb of God. The *Litany of the Saints* is sung at the Easter Vigil and various sacramental rites, and litanies are commonly used in devotions.

Intercessory litanies should have a sense of urgency. The petitions we present are important and pressing. Usually the music for litanies is quite simple, an apt vehicle for ritual sung prayer. The verses usually end with a set cue phrase (i.e. *We pray to the Lord*) so that the assembly clearly knows when to respond. Because the invocations are short and the response frequent, litanies develop a rhythm. This can be made even more urgent if the assembly's response slightly overlaps the cantor's cue phrase, and the cantors next invocation begins before the response has faded. This overlapping cycle promotes urgency and a sense of incompleteness which can only be satisfied by God's reply.

More settings are becoming available for singing the general intercessions and other litanies. The most commonly used setting of the text *Lord, hear our prayer* is in *Worship* #240. Other responses can be found in *Worship* #296-300 and *Gather* #74, 123-125.

SELECTING REPERTOIRE

The musical settings for hymns and songs, acclamations, responses, responsorial music, and litanies need to be chosen carefully. Cantors may or may not have the responsibility of selecting or suggesting the music to be sung by the parish. In any event, it is important that cantors understand the basic principles of choosing music for worship. Acclamations should be used for a long period of time, becoming part of the instinctive repertoire of the parish assembly. Therefore, it is critically important that the acclamations be pieces that will retain their interest. Building a body of songs familiar to everyone demands time and patience, so it is important that the energy goes into good selections.

Three Judgements

The booklet *Music in Catholic Worship* is basic reading for any pastoral musician. It identifies three judgements which should be applied to each piece of music considered for use in liturgies:

> **Musical**—Is the music technically, aesthetically, and expressively good? (no. 26)
> **Liturgical**—The nature of the liturgy itself will help to determine what kind of music is called for, what parts are to be preferred for singing, and who is to sing them. (no. 30)
> **Pastoral**—Does music in the celebration enable these people to express their faith, in this place, in this age, in this culture? (no. 39)

There is a great quantity of published liturgical music available today. The quality of compositions has improved in recent years, especially the quality of the texts. While much of the music is of excellent quality, much does not meet the standard of the three judgements. Publication does not assure that pieces are good musically, liturgically, or pastorally. Of the pieces that are good musically, some are appropriate for liturgy at properly selected points in the rite. Of the pieces left, those selected must be good pastorally, that is, helpful to the expression of the faith of the people in this particular community. Pastoral judgements will vary, even within a city or diocese. Independent judgement is necessary.

Knowing about the music publishers can be helpful. Some companies generally produce reliable music. Others are not as dependable.

Music that is not formally published often deserves the same consideration as published materials, but it should also be scrutinized in light of the three judgements. It may be necessary for parish musicians to compose antiphons for specific occasions. This is good, but it is necessary to be objective in deciding to use such pieces.

Music is available in hymnals and songbooks, at book and gift stores (especially those oriented to Catholics, Episcopals, and Lutherans), and by direct mail from the publishers. A selected list of publishers is included in Appendix 2. They will all send catalogs upon request.

SINGING THE PSALMS

The Book of Psalms is the traditional songbook for Jews and Christians. Liturgically, we think most often of the responsorial psalm of the Mass, but psalms are also the basis of the texts of many of the hymns and songs we sing. Psalms provide the bulk of the Liturgy of the Hours.

The full texts of the psalms are found in the Bible. The Lectionary provides selected, edited psalms for each Sunday and weekday, as well as seasonal psalms which may be substituted for the day's given psalm.

There are several commonly used methods for singing the psalms. These include psalm tones, the compositions by Joseph Gelineau, metrical settings, and through-composed versions (which do not repeat a melody from one verse to the next and are sung straight through by the cantor).

Psalm Tones

The psalm tones are chant melodic formulas to which the psalms may be sung. They are convenient, because a melody may be used for many different texts. There are several traditional psalm tones which may be found in the *Liber usualis,* the collection of Gregorian chants in standard use before the Second Vatican Council. Many new chants have also been composed.

Psalm tone 8g, which is probably the best known, gives a good example of the structure and style of the psalm tones.

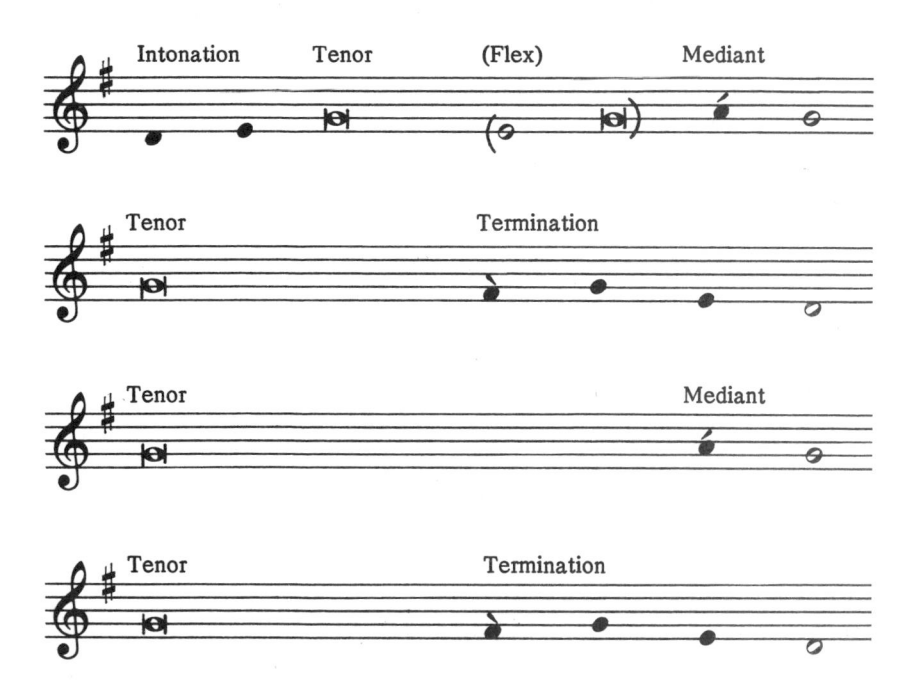

[Musical notation: Four staves showing the psalm tone 8g structure]

Line 1: Intonation — Tenor — (Flex) — Mediant
Line 2: Tenor — Termination
Line 3: Tenor — Mediant
Line 4: Tenor — Termination

These formula melodies usually begin with a short *intonation* pattern (see example) followed by a pitch called the *tenor* (from the Latin word *tenere*, to hold) to which most of the words are sung. If the line is long enough to require two breaths, the *flex* (denoted by –) is used on an important word. After a breath, the singer resumes the *tenor* pitch until the line ends with the *mediant* (denoted by ´). The second line begins with the *tenor* and concludes with the *termination* formula (marked `, usually four syllables from the end of the line). The second two lines follow the same pattern, except that the *intonation* is omitted. Line three begins on the *tenor* pitch.

Here is part of Psalm 24(25) from the First Sunday of Advent, Year C, set to tone 8g, and written in modern notation. Be aware that the notes are placed in groups of two or three. These groupings give chant a rhythmic structure. Even in the traditional Gregorian notation, these groupings of two and three apply, although this is not obvious to the musician who has not studied chant.

Lord, make me know your ways. Lord, teach me your paths.

Make me walk in your truth and teach me, for you are

God my Sav-ior. In you I hope all day long.

© 1963, The Grail

The symbols (‾, ´, `) used to show the various melodic patterns are called *points*. *Pointing* the psalm text makes it unnecessary to write out the music for each line of the psalm. Here is a pointed version of the same psalm.

    Lord, make me knów your ways.

    Lord, tèach me your paths.

    Make me walk in your truth, and teach mē

        for you are God my sávior.

    In you I hòpe all day long.

This system is a very practical type of shorthand. You may want to mark your own copy of the Lectionary or psalter. The psalms and canticles (other biblical songs) in *Worship* (#24-99) are already pointed.

The psalm tones were traditionally used with texts in Latin. English does not employ the same phrase structure as Latin, so subtle adaptations must be made at times. One common change is to sing the last syllable of a line to two pitches. It is possible that different cantors will make different correct decisions.

If a psalm tone is used for the verses of the responsorial psalm, a metrical setting of the antiphon is most often paired with it. If you are selecting the musical combination, be sure to match the mode of the verses and antiphon.

In all cases, the rhythm follows the pattern of speech. The most common mistake in the performance of psalm tones is to take them too slowly, especially at the ends of lines where the melodic formula changes. The way to solve this is to read the text first, with good interpretation. What are the important words? What thoughts are being conveyed? How does the text fit into rhythmic groupings of twos and threes? Be careful with diction. *These melodies aren't interesting. What matters is the text.* If it cannot be understood, meaning is lost. If psalm tones are sung with care, the psalms can come alive as poetry and prayer. If not, they will be boring and mechanical.

Gelineau

Joseph Gelineau is a French priest, liturgist, and composer. He pioneered a style of psalm settings which has a steady pulse, one pulse per measure. Within each measure of the verses, various numbers of syllables are sung, following the pattern of speech. The psalm translations are based on the rhythm of the original Hebrew texts, which have three stresses per line. The Gelineau psalms are published with antiphons by various composers. The underlying pulse of the psalm verses remains constant in the antiphon. Other composers have adopted this style at times, but Gelineau's psalm settings are the landmark, and all cantors should be familiar with them. Here is Gelineau's Psalm 50(51) (*Worship* #41).

Antiphon 1 — Joseph Gelineau, SJ

Have mer-cy, Lord, cleanse me from all my sins.

(Mode: Ray. Tonic: D)

1. Have mercy on me, God, in your kindness.
2. My of-fenses truly I know them;
3. That you may be justified when you give sentence
4. In-deed you love truth in the heart;

1. In your com-passion blot out my óf-fense.
2. my sin is always bé-fore me.
3. and be with-out re-proach when yóu judge,
4. then in the secret of my heart teach mé wisdom.

1. O wash me more and more from mý guilt
2. Against you, you a-lone, have I sinned;
3. O see, in guilt I wàs born,
4. O purify me, then I shall bè clean;

1. and cleanse me from mý sin.
2. what is evil in your sight I háve done.
3. a sinner was I cón-ceived.
4. O wash, me, I shall be whiter thán snow.

© 1963, The Grail

In performance these psalm settings can be accompanied by either keyboard or guitar (see Appendix 2 for a list of scores).

Metrical Settings

The term *metrical* can have two meanings. One refers to the practice of paraphrasing the text of a psalm so that it fits into a particular poetic meter. This became popular during the Reformation and many metrical psalms are in use today, including "All People That on Earth Do Dwell" (*Worship* #669).

Musical settings of psalms can also be metrical, as opposed to the rhythmic flexibility allowed in chant or within the measures of Gelineau's psalms. The text may or may not be in a strict poetic meter, but the rhythm of every note is written out. A wealth of settings have become available in recent years in all styles. Much of today's best-known liturgical music uses psalm texts either directly or in paraphrase, even though they may not be identified as such.

THE EXSULTET

The Easter Proclamation, or *Exsultet,* deserves special mention. It is sung at the Easter Vigil, immediately after the procession into the church with the paschal candle. This long, beautiful chant, which traces the history of salvation, can be sung by a cantor as well as a priest or deacon. Most priests will gladly ask a good cantor to sing it because of its length, difficulty, and beauty. What a privilege it is to sing this annual proclamation to an Easter assembly glowing with candle light! If you have the opportunity to sing the *Exsultet,* reserve enough time for careful practice. The complete music can be found in the Sacramentary. Robert Batastini has adapted another version (see Appendix 2).

7. Helping People Sing

This book, which is subtitled "Helping Catholics Pray in Song," concentrates on the role of the cantor. There are some matters which, while they may not fall under the direct responsibility of cantors, will be covered here because they help to build musical participation.

Once I wrote an article for the Seattle archdiocesan newspaper's "Liturgy Page." The headline I submitted was "Helping People Sing." I realize that was not a particularly catchy title. However, for space reasons, and probably to draw some attention, the editor changed the title to "Why Don't People Sing in Church?" This headline implied that it is the assembly's fault for not singing. However, I believe it is too easy for pastoral musicians to blame the congregation for lack of musical participation. I sincerely feel that most people *will* sing under good circumstances. Often, it is we musicians and other ministers who, unwittingly, stand in the way.

Here are my suggestions.

HOSPITALITY

The members of the community should be well aware that we musicians welcome their song. This can be communicated by an inviting cantor, attractive and practical worship aids (which contain both words and music), and clear instructions (visual and/or aural) about where to find any words or music needed. If musicians have an attitude of inhospitality and indifference to the people's involvement in the music, the people will sense this. It's easy to see when someone is a *performer* and not a *minister*. They prefer to have people listen instead of joining in, and they communicate that message in clear, nonverbal signals. In this case, the motives and pastoral sense of the musician need immediate attention.

MUSICAL QUALITY

Nobody wants to sing a song that is trite, simplistic, or boring. Careful music selection based on quality is mandatory. Do not ignore the text. While the melody is an important component, the text is the direct carrier of the message. Obviously, the quality of the performance by the musicians must also be the highest possible.

SINGABILITY

Be sure the song is singable. This may be terribly obvious, but many people in liturgy and music do not always make careful choices of songs for everyone to sing. Many hymns which are perfect for conventions of musicians are not well suited for parish use. Check the range. Soaring to the heights or plummeting to very low pitches is fine for a trained choir, but not for average people. A range of a ninth or tenth, from B-flat up to C or D is a safe range. Singing beyond that practical limit is possible in theory but only occasionally in fact. Many people will be left out.

Tempos and rhythms are critical. The slow tempo of a dirge is exhausting for most people. Don't go too slowly. Too brisk a tempo is a less frequent problem, but it also can be troublesome. Intricate or syncopated rhythms will often cause difficulties. Congregations will often simplify them. Pieces which have many rhythmic variations among the verses are awkward for those who don't read music. It may be best to leave the parts with intricate, syncopated, or varied rhythms to the choir.

CONSISTENCY

Liturgical music is *ritual* music. This means that many musical parts will not need to be changed from week to week. Consistency is a major factor in improving musical participation. People feel more comfortable when they know which parts of the Mass are usually sung. Repetition and reinforcement will help people to know the music so well that it is easily sung, much of it from memory.

I am convinced that a consistent program of good music will not bore people. Acclamations and responses should be changed infrequently. Two new settings in a year is the most I recommend. Once a repertoire of three or four sets of well-known acclamations is developed, it is possible to change the settings with the seasons, perhaps introducing a new set only annually.

The responsorial psalm presents a unique challenge. It is ideal to sing the given psalm because of its connection with the first reading. If the parish consistently uses one source for the psalms, all of the refrains will have been sung over the three-year Lectionary cycle. They are then repeated, reinforcing them over a long time span. If this is too demanding, especially at first, it is possible to sing seasonal psalms. Texts are provided in the Lectionary and musical collections of them have been published. Using the same antiphon over several weeks allows it to be easily learned and well sung. The seasonal verses may be used each week or the given psalm verses for the Sunday can be adapted for use with the antiphon.

Using one or two hymns during an entire season gives people a chance to learn them well. A *hymn-of-the-month* is a similar idea. Sometimes a theme continues over several weeks in the Lectionary. In the Seventeenth through the Twentieth Sundays of Ordinary Time in Year B, the gospel is drawn from the sixth chapter of John, which highlights the eucharist. That would be a good time to select a new eucharistic hymn and sing it each Sunday for the four weeks.

The only complaints I have ever heard about this consistent kind of programing have come from the choir. Because they have rehearsal and attend one Mass very regularly, they hear the music much more than the congregation. It is important for choir members to understand that this is part of their ministry. The choir and the assembly will get variety with changes in hymns and pieces for the choir.

TEACHING

It seems highly inhospitable for people to be expected to sing a song they've never heard before. If we want them to sing, we must help them become familiar with the music.

Often-used methods for teaching music to a congregation include having the choir or the organ perform the piece for a number of Sundays before the whole assembly is invited to sing it. However, I don't think that approach always works well. The direct teaching of a new song can provide much better results.

Music teaching can be done in two or three minutes maximum, in the time before the opening song. It need not be a half-hour lesson if the material is prepared carefully by the cantor. In my experience, unaccompanied singing teaches best. This allows people to really hear how they sound and enables the cantor to listen for problem areas.

This is the method I use. The cantor and/or choir sing through the entire piece, possibly this time with accompaniment, so that people get a sense of it. Then the cantor sings one phrase and asks everyone to repeat it, unaccompanied. Then the second phrase is sung and repeated, and so forth. Following this pattern, the entire song can be learned quickly. Conducting, using the *pitch/rhythm* method outlined earlier can be very helpful in teaching a new piece.

Some cautions. Correct blatant mistakes, but do not be too meticulous. It makes no sense to reinforce notes that are very far from correct, but leave well enough alone if people are on the right track. Unnecessary persistence will be irksome.

Talk as little as possible. Hand signals can cue the assembly's repetitions and save a great deal of time. It may help to learn the music at a slower tempo than the final one. Don't be condescending. Even little things can give a wrong message. Say, "We will *learn* this today" rather than "I'm going to *teach* you this song today."

Of course, these rehearsals will be most effective if all of the ministers take part, including the presider.

Another very practical method can be used for acclamations if your parishioners, like those in many places, arrive exactly on time or even a little late. In this case a rehearsal beforehand is not effective, so at the proper time during Mass the cantor alone sings the acclamation (or, if it is long, the first section of it). Then everyone repeats, following the pattern until the piece is finished. After three or four weeks, the music is well known and the repeats can be eliminated. This has worked well for me and my parishes.

ACOUSTICS AND ARRANGEMENT

Most cantors will not be able to change either the arrangement of their church building or its acoustics. However, be aware that these two factors make an enormous difference in the assembly's participation. Seating arrangements which let people see each other encourage and facilitate singing. The support of other people singing encourages the reticent ones to take part.

Acoustics can make or break a music program in a parish, especially in the area of community participation. "Dead" rooms are not called that by accident. In such spaces, sounds die as soon as they are made instead of being alive in the space until they fade naturally. Acoustical tile, excess carpeting, and large amounts of soft wood absorb sound quickly.

The all-too-common practice of carpeting the entire floor of the worship space has a ruinous effect on liturgical music. It's that simple. A competent acoustical engineer who understands Catholic liturgy and music will be able to balance the room's reverberation for ease of both speaking and singing. There must be lively reverberation to support hearty congregational singing—period!

INSTRUMENTS AND AMPLIFICATION

It is difficult to sing with instruments that are inadequate to the space or in poor repair. A small piano or organ suited for a home simply cannot do the job of leading several hundred participants. Many organs installed before Vatican II were designed to accompany a small chant schola, not mixed choirs and congregational hymns. The sound amplification systems in many churches are geared to the speaking voice, not music. They cannot faithfully reproduce the full range of musical sound, but are limited to the middle range. As a result, even good music can sound bad.

Both of these problems are easily solved, but at some cost. Fine instruments, well-suited to liturgical use, are available. Sound systems which can amplify both music and the spoken word well are being installed in many churches. The sound needs to be appropriate to the space and natural. Good amplification is not necessarily louder, just more faithful to the full range of sound.

START WITH ACCLAMATIONS

If you need to start from scratch in helping your parish learn to sing, start small, and start with the liturgical priorities. Give top priority to the acclamations. The acclamations are short and usually easily sung. Since they are changed infrequently, the assembly will have a good chance to hear and get to know them.

Instead of using hymns which must be sung in their entirety, use antiphonal psalms and songs. A two to four bar refrain is easier to master than longer pieces. For longer songs, stick with the most familiar of traditional hymns at the beginning.

Remember the goal of teaching music to a parish assembly. The singing is to help people pray and share in the celebration. Building repertoire should not become a quest in itself outside this primary goal. Time and patience will be needed.

8. The Parish Cantor Program

LITURGIES OTHER THAN THE SUNDAY MASS

The role of cantor exists because the worshiping community has a need for musical leadership and encouragement. That need goes beyond the parish Sunday Mass. Music is an integral part of our communal prayer life, and cantors have an important role in making that happen in the variety of liturgies in the parish. Music is designed into our rituals for baptism, marriage, funerals, the Rite of Christian Initiation of Adults, communal reconciliation, and morning and evening prayer.

The cantor is not just a soloist at these liturgies. The role is the same as at Mass: proclamation of the psalm and animation of the assembly's musical participation. In some parishes, this means a big change. The congregation, still used to being musically passive at liturgies other than the eucharist is now asked to take an active part. The wedding changes from liturgical pageant to prayerful celebration by all present. While there is still a place for beautiful vocal solos, the musical focus will be on the assembly. Bringing this norm into practice requires a commitment on the part of musicians and other liturgical ministers, especially the presider, and education and formation of those who are to take part in the liturgies.

This book is intended to assist inexperienced cantors and those who train them. The Sunday Mass is the place to begin, so a detailed examination of liturgies other than the eucharist is not included here. Specific information about particular liturgies can be found in the rites themselves.

QUALITY BEFORE QUANTITY

Maybe you have been, and will be, the one and only cantor for your parish. However, the ideal is to carefully develop a group of cantors who can give their time and talents to meet the variety of needs of parish worship. Some parishes have no trouble finding people who have good voices, are at ease in front of people, and are willing to serve. Other communities will have to search resourcefully, giving careful training to potential cantors. They may have to be hired from outside the parish.

Always seek quality before quantity. The parish will be better served by fewer persons who are well qualified than by a crowd of volunteers long on goodwill and short on basic qualifications. It is difficult to turn down people who want to help, but the music director must have the ability and the support to do so in order to maintain a credible ministry to the whole community. Willing but unqualified persons need and deserve special effort to direct their energies into other areas of parish ministry.

TWO CANTORS

At times it may be advantageous to use two cantors at once during a liturgy. When there is a solo part which alternates with a congregational refrain, such as in responsorial-form pieces or litanies, one cantor can be the vocal soloist while the other leads the response. If the assembly is divided antiphonally, this is, from side-to-side, a cantor for each side makes it easier for everyone to be comfortable singing at the correct time. This is especially crucial if a round or echo part is being sung by the entire congregation.

TRAINING AND REHEARSALS

Cantors must be carefully trained before they begin their ministry with the assembly. This may be done one-on-one, in parish groups, or at diocesan or other programs. See Appendix 3 for training exercises. Once cantors are functioning in their ministry, brush-up and support sessions are important. Meetings can be used for learning new music, especially the responsorial psalms, and for group practice and critique. Evaluation—by the music director, instrumentalists, and other cantor colleagues—can be an invaluable tool for growth and development when used in a supportive and positive way. Reasonable efforts should be made to encourage a social and friendly relationship among cantors and other members of the music team. Potluck suppers, wine and cheese gatherings, and other events are important for building a common purpose, a sense of ministry, and mutual support.

Video taping is very helpful for new cantors as they begin to learn their skills. Even experienced cantors will benefit from watching themselves. This allows objective self-analysis. Nothing is more revealing or helpful.

Learning new music can be time consuming, especially with cantors who do not read music well. I have saved a lot of time by recording simple piano and voice versions of the upcoming two-to-three months of responsorial psalms. The cantors can listen to the tape at their convenience. As a result, even cantors who are unable to read music have always been prepared when they came to rehearsal, and their confidence was greater because they knew the music well.

WORKING WITH OTHER MUSICIANS

Cantors must rehearse carefully with other musicians until a working dynamic is set. Questions about time lags (such as when the organ is in the back), acoustics, and cues can be worked out. Everyone will need to become acquainted musically, learning about the peculiarities of each other's musical style and technique. Each church building and pastoral musician is unique, so use common sense, patience, and lots of time.

APPEARANCE

No uniform standards can be set for the apparel of cantors, but good judgement will answer any questions that arise. The clothes of the cantor must be appropriate to the community gathered to pray. *Appropriate* can range from formal suits and dresses to sportswear or jeans. The circumstances and common sense determine what is best.

Should cantors wear vestments? I generally do not, but in some situations an alb or other vestment may be helpful in adding a sense of festivity or special dignity to a given celebration. Whether or not a robe is worn is not nearly as important as a clear rationale for doing so, or not doing so. Wearing a robe simply to draw attention is never acceptable. It seems reasonable, however, that if one group of lay ministers wears vesture, a*ll* should. The unfortunate practice of eucharistic ministers being vested when no other lay ministers are is a signal of a hierarchical structure among the ministries which is not appropriate. Cantors should not promote such a situation with their own dress.

Part of appropriate appearance is the way in which cantors hold their printed music materials. A simple, attractive folder helps avoid the disheveled look which often occurs when holding many books and papers. To avoid shuffling paper during Mass, materials should be put in order within your folder beforehand.

PAYMENT

The issue of payment for professional or very competent ministry services to the parish is a matter that could be explored in great detail, particularly regarding musicians. Like other experienced musicians, a cantor spends much time and money in personal training and needs to give much time in preparation for parish worship services.

I see three groups among pastoral musicians, delineated by their competence and experience. The first group includes the degreed musician who earns a livelihood from music, either full- or part-time, and views it as a profession. The second takes in the skilled amateur who has studied for many years and may continue to do so, at great cost of time and money. This musician does not depend on pastoral music as the primary source of income, but it may be an important secondary income. The third group is made up of willing parishioners who have musical talent, in whatever stage of development, and want to share it with the community. All three are vital in pastoral music. All parishes must have the last two and strong programs require all three.

Each parish must decide on a policy about pay for musicians. It is always better to decide this question objectively, before the situation arises, because this removes concern about specific individuals from the decision-making process.

It is my opinion that people in the first two groups, the degreed professional and the highly trained amateur, should always be paid. The Church must support those who earn their livelihood in service to it, as well as those who pay or have paid for lessons to develop their skills to a high level, when that is required by the community. I believe that this payment should be automatic, on the basis of parish policy. Then, if a particular musician wishes to donate part or all of the remuneration back to the parish, that is the musician's free choice.

The third group should not be paid. This is volunteer service as with most other ministries. If, however, those in this group need private voice study to be effective cantors, the parish would do well to help pay for the lessons.

Because this varies so widely, I hesitate to offer specific suggestions about the appropriate amount of pay. Parishes and geographic areas have differing standards. Discussion with comparable parishes or the diocesan music office should offer guidance.

The question of money makes pastors, parish councils, and parishioners nervous, and it is no easier on cantors and other music ministers. Cantors should help in the process by establishing their basic fee and by not portraying themselves as ignorant or noncommittal on the matter of money. It is a common and awkward habit of good-willed, ministry-oriented people to indicate a disinterest in money, even when it is important to their livelihood. This mannerism places an unreasonable burden on the people responsible for equitable distribution of parish money. The direct method, respectfully handled, earns respect in return and builds trust.

COMMISSIONING

As with other parish ministers, it is good to recognize and support the service of cantors to the community by commissioning their ministry formally and publicly in a liturgical celebration. The celebration might include a brief explanation of the ministry, a commissioning prayer, the laying on of hands, and the presentation of an appropriate gift or symbol of the ministry (a medallion, pin, or book of the psalms). The formal recognition of the direct relationship between the community and the cantor will help to solidify that relationship. The bond between cantor and assembly is vital and should be nurtured.

9. CONCLUSION

BE YOURSELF

One last practical note. In this book I have outlined numerous principles, priorities, and techniques for cantors to master. The tasks of the ministry can be fulfilled in many different ways and with varied personal styles. Every good cantor will find that unique way of doing things which is personal and natural. Ten good cantors will do things ten different ways, and that is good. You can only be yourself, not a clone of someone else.

Even with the best of preparation, mistakes will happen. They can be caused by last-minute changes of plans, forgetfulness, or just nervousness. Cantors must be ready to be flexible and make the best of the situation in a dignified way. A curious dynamic seems to happen in these tense situations. If the assembly has developed a relationship of trust and affection for the cantor—and this should happen—infrequent mistakes will be seen only as slightly humorous and somewhat endearing. People really do like to see our humanity. Such episodes tell people that the cantor is one of them. You know the old line about *laughing at* and *laughing with*. Obviously, this is not to be confused with incompetence or laziness, which are never humorous or endearing.

FINALLY...

In the ten years since the writing of the first edition of this book, many more parishes have cantors leading them in prayerful song. The repertoire we have to sing has been expanded and improved. The *folk group,* which was quite limited in its musical range, has grown and broadened into a *contemporary music group* or *choir* which uses more instruments and expanded vocal parts. Mixed choirs flourish in many parishes, keeping alive the Catholic musical heritage while growing with the times. And, most importantly, the assembly's own song has developed. A common repertoire of good quality has begun to emerge. There is surely room for continued growth, but there is now a good foundation and common understanding of the general direction we follow.

As cantors we take part in that growth and lead the emerging song of the God's people. Cantors can make a difference as we strive, as Catholic communities, to pray in song. It is hard work—a challenge and a privilege.

APPENDIX 1
INSTRUCTIONS FOR CANTORS FROM OFFICIAL DOCUMENTS

All texts in brackets were added by the author. They do not appear in the official documents.

GENERAL INSTRUCTION OF THE ROMAN MISSAL (1975)

26. The entrance song is sung alternately by the choir and the congregation or by the cantor and the congregation; or it is sung entirely by the congregation or the choir alone.

30. Then the Kyrie begins, unless it has already been included as a part of the penitential rite. Since it is a song by which the faithful praise the Lord and implore his mercy, it is ordinarily prayed by all, that is, alternately by the congregation and the choir or cantor.

36. The psalmist or cantor of the [responsorial] psalm sings the verses of the psalm at the lectern or other suitable place. The people remain seated and listen, but also as a rule take part by singing the response, except when the psalm is sung straight through without the response.

37. The Alleluia is sung in every season outside Lent. It is begun by all present or by the choir or cantor; it may then be repeated. [In the most common U.S. pastoral practice, the cantor sings the alleluia, which is repeated by all.]

47. It is desirable that a deacon, cantor, or other person announce the intentions [of the general intercessions]. [Notice the listed order; the Missal prefers the cantor to a lector.]

56. Agnus Dei: during the breaking of the bread and the commingling, the Agnus Dei is as a rule sung by the choir or cantor with the congregation responding; otherwise it is recited aloud. This invocation may be repeated as often as necessary to accompany the breaking of the bread. The final reprise concludes with the words, "grant us peace."

56. During the priest's and the faithful's reception of the sacrament the communion song is sung...by the choir alone or by the choir or cantor with the congregation.

63. The *schola cantorum* or choir exercises its own liturgical function within the assembly. Its task is to ensure that the parts proper to it, in keeping with the different types of chants, are carried out becomingly

and to encourage active participation of the people in the singing. What is said about the choir applies in a similar way to other musicians, especially the organist.

64. There should be a cantor or a choir director to lead and sustain the people in singing. When in fact there is no choir, it is up to the cantor to lead the various songs, and the people take part in the way proper to them.

67. The cantor of the psalm is to sing the psalm or other biblical song that comes between the readings. To fulfill their function correctly, these cantors should possess singing talent and an aptitutde for correct pronunciation and diction.

77. As far as possible, and especially on Sundays and holydays of obligation, this Mass should be celebrated with song and with a suitable number of ministers. But it may be celebrated without music and with only one minister.

78. It is desirable that as a rule an acolyte, a reader, and a cantor assist the priest celebrant.

87. After the penitential act, the Kyrie and Gloria are said, in keeping with the rubrics (no. 30-31). Either the priest or the cantors or even everyone together may begin the Gloria.

90. After the [first] reading, the psalmist or cantor of the psalm, or even the reader sings or recites the psalm and the congregation sings or recites the response (see no. 36).

150. If there is no cantor of the psalm, [the reader] may also sing or recite the responsorial psalm after the first reading.

272. The readings, responsorial psalm, and the Easter Proclamation (Exsultet) are proclaimed from the lectern; it may be used also for the homily and general intercessions (prayer of the faithful). It is better for the commentator, cantor, or choir director not to use the lectern. [The cantor uses another visible location from which to lead singing, except for the psalm, Exsultet, and the general intercessions.]

THE ROMAN MISSAL [THE "SACRAMENTARY"] (1985)

[These instructions are from the rubrics printed in the Order of Mass]

Penitential Rite C. The priest (or other suitable minister) makes the following or other invocations: You were sent to heal the contrite: Lord, have mercy. [The cantor would be a "suitable minister" if these invocations and responses are sung.]

Responsorial Psalm. The cantor sings or recites the psalm, and the people respond.

General Intercessions. It is desirable that the intentions be announced by the deacon, cantor, or other person. [Note that the lector is not specified.]

APPENDIX TO THE GENERAL INSTRUCTION FOR THE DIOCESES OF THE UNITED STATES OF AMERICA (1985)

66. d) Other ministries performed by women, such as leading the singing or otherwise directing the congregation, should be done either within or outside the sanctuary area, depending on circumstances or conveniences.

DIRECTORY FOR MASSES WITH CHILDREN (1973)

22. Every effort should...be made to increase this participation and to make it more intense. For this reason as many children as possible should have special parts in the celebration: for example, preparing the place and the altar, acting as cantor, singing in a choir, playing musical instruments, proclaiming the readings, responding during the homily, reciting the intentions of the general intercessions, bringing the gifts to the altar, and performing similar activities in accord with the usage of various communities.
24. Even with Masses with children attention is to be paid to the diversity of ministries so that the Mass may stand out clearly as the celebration of a community. For example, readers and cantors, whether children or adults, should be employed.

MUSIC IN CATHOLIC WORSHIP (1983)

35. The Cantor. While there is no place in the liturgy for display of virtuosity for its own sake, artistry is valued, and an individual singer can effectively lead the assembly, attractively proclaim the Word of God in the psalm sung between the readings, and take his or her part in other responsorial singing. "Provision should be made for at least one or two properly trained singers, especially where there is no possibility of setting up even a small choir. The singer will present some simpler musical settings, with the people taking part, and can lead and support the faithful as far as is needed. The presence of such a singer is desirable even in churches which have a choir, for those celebrations in which the choir cannot take part, but which may fittingly be performed with some solemnity and therefore with singing" [Congregation of Rites, Instruction of Music in the Liturgy,

Musicam Sacram, March 5, 1967, no. 21]. Although a cantor "cannot enhance the service of worship in the same way as a choir, a trained and competent cantor can perform an important ministry by leading the congregation in common sacred song and in responsorial singing" [Bishops' Committee on the Liturgy, April 18, 1966]

77. The Church in the United States today needs the services of many qualified musicians as song leaders, organists, instrumentalists, cantors, choir directors, and composers. We have been blessed with many generous musicians who have given years of service despite receiving only meager financial compensation. For the art to grow and face the challenges of today and tomorrow, every diocese and parish should establish policies for hiring and paying living wages to competent musicians. Full-time musicians employed by the Church ought to be on the same salary scale as teachers with similar qualifications and workloads [Bishops' Committee on the Liturgy, April 18, 1966]. [Given the widespread injustice of the pay scales of Catholic grade school teachers, public school salaries might represent a fairer comparison.]

LITURGICAL MUSIC TODAY (1982)

1. In the liturgical ministry of music, more and more capable persons are assuming roles of leadership as cantors, instrumentalists and members of choirs.

32. Many parishes have found it helpful to form choirs...whose unique ministry it is to assist the grieving members of a funeral assembly by leading the sung prayer of the funeral liturgy. Where this is not possible, a cantor is able to perform a similar ministry. In all cases a serious effort should be made to move beyond the practice of employing a "funeral singer" to perform all the sung parts of the liturgy. Reconsideration should be given to the location of the singer, that person's role, and the kind of music that is sung. The cantor ought not individually sing or recite the congregational prayers as a substitute for the assembly.

68. Among music ministers, the cantor has come to be recognized as having a crucial role in the development of congregational singing. Besides being qualified to lead singing, he or she must have the skills to introduce and teach new music, and to encourage the assembly. This must be done with sensitivity so that the cantor does not intrude on the communal prayer or become manipulative. Introductions and announcements should be brief and avoid a homiletic style.

69. The cantor's role is distinct from that of the psalmist, whose

ministry is the singing of the verses of the responsorial psalm and communion psalm. Frequently the two roles will be combined in one person.

INTRODUCTION TO THE LECTIONARY FOR MASS (1981)

19. The responsorial psalm, also called the gradual, has great liturgical and pastoral significance because it is "an integral part of the liturgy of the word" [General Instruction of the Roman Missal, no. 36]. Accordingly, the people must be continually instructed on the way to perceive the word of God speaking in the psalms and to turn these psalms into the prayer of the Church....A brief remark may be helpful about the choice of psalm and response as well as their correspondence to the readings.

20. As a rule the responsorial psalm should be sung. There are two established ways of singing the psalm after the first reading: responsorially or directly. In responsorial singing, which, as far as possible, is to be given preference, the psalmist or cantor of the psalm sings the psalm verse and the whole congregation joins in by singing the response. In direct singing of the psalm there is no intervening response by the community; either the psalmist or cantor of the psalm sings the psalm alone as the community listens or else all sing it together.

21. The singing of the psalm, or even of the response alone, is a great help toward understanding and meditating on the psalm's spiritual meaning.

To foster the congregation's singing, every means available in the various cultures is to be employed. In particular use is to be made of all the relevant options provided in the Order of Readings for Mass regarding responses corresponding to the different liturgical seasons.

22. When not sung, the psalm after the reading is to be recited in a manner conducive to meditation on the word of God.

The responsorial psalm is sung or recited by the psalmist or cantor at the lectern.

23. The Alleluia or, as the liturgical season requires, the verse before the gospel, is also a "rite or act standing by itself" [See General Instruction of the Roman Missal, no. 39]. It serves as the assembled faithful's greeting of welcome to the Lord who is about to speak to them and as an expression of their faith through song.

The Alleluia or the verse before the gospel must be sung and during it all stand. It is not to be sung only by the cantor who intones it or by the choir, but by the whole congregation together.

30. The celebrant introduces the prayer [General Intercessions]; the deacon, another minister, or some of the faithful may propose intentions that are short and phrased with a measure of flexibility.

31. The congregation takes part in the general intercessions while standing and by saying or singing a common response after each intention or by silent prayer.

33. Since the lectern is the place from which the ministers proclaim the word of God, it must of its nature be reserved for the readings, the responsorial psalm, and the Easter proclamation *(Exsultet)*. The lectern may rightly be used for the homily and the general intercessions, however, because of their close connection with the entire liturgy of the word. It is better for the commentator, cantor, or director of singing, for example, not to use the lectern.

56. The psalmist, that is the cantor of the psalm, is responsible for singing, responsorially or directly, the chants between the readings—the psalm or other biblical canticle, the gradual and Alleluia, or other chant. The psalmist may, as occasion requires, intone the Alleluia and verse.

For carrying out the function of psalmist it is advantageous to have in each ecclesial community laypersons with a talent for singing and correct diction. The points made about the formation of readers apply to cantors as well. [This refers to no. 52 of these instructions: "The liturgical assembly truly requires readers, even those not instituted. Proper measures must therefore be taken to ensure that there are qualified laypersons who have been trained to carry out this ministry."]

APPENDIX 2.
RESOURCES FOR CANTORS

BOOKS AND PERIODICALS

Carroll, J. R. *Guide to Gelineau Psalmody*. Chicago: GIA, 1979.
Hansen, James. *The Ministry of the Cantor*. Collegeville, MN: The Liturgical Press, 1985.
Huck, Gabe. *How Can I Keep From Singing?* Chicago: Liturgy Training Publications, 1989.
Huijbers, Bernard. *The Performing Audience*. 2nd ed. Phoenix: North American Liturgy Resources, 1980.
Johnson, Lawrence J. *The Ministers of Music*. Washington: National Association of Pastoral Musicians, 1983.
Kodner Sotak, Diana. *Handbook for Cantors*. Chicago: Liturgical Training Publications, 1988.
Leaver, Robin A., David Mann, and David Parkes, ed. *Ways of Singing the Psalms*. London: Collins Liturgical Publications, 1984.
Pastoral Music. Published six times annually by the National Association of Pastoral Musicians, 225 Sheridan St. NW, Washington, DC 20011-1492. Two issues are of particular interest to cantors: Vol. 4, No. 1 (October–November 1979) devoted to *The Animator: Exploring a New Liturgical Role;* and Vol. 14, No. 4 (April–May 1990) featuring *Congregational Participation*.

CANTOR TRAINING

Brownstead, Frank. *Cantoring: A Video Notebook*. Washington: The Pastoral Press, 1990.
Hansen, James. *Training the Parish Cantor*. Collegeville, MN: The Liturgical Press, 1991. A training video.
Marcheschi, Graziano with Nancy Seitz Marcheschi. *Workbook for Lectors and Gospel Readers*. Chicago: Liturgy Training Publications, published annually. The readings are marked for stresses and pauses. Excellent for practicing interpretation.
NPM School for Cantors and Lectors. National Association of Pastoral Musicians, 225 Sheridan St. NW, Washington, DC 20011-1492. Several sessions held around the U.S. each summer.

OFFICIAL DOCUMENTS

Lectionary, The. New York: Catholic Book Publishing Co., 1970.
Order of Christian Funerals. Collegeville: Liturgical Press, 1989.
Rite of Christian Initiation of Adults. Chicago: Liturgy Training Publications, 1988.
Rites of the Catholic Church, The. New York: Pueblo Publishing Co., 197 , 1980. These two volumes are now available through The Liturgical Press.
Sacramentary, The. New York: Catholic Book Publishing Co., 1974. This is the *Roman Missal* which contains the Order of Mass.
Simcoe, Mary Ann, ed. *The Liturgy Documents: A Parish Resource.* 2nd ed. Chicago: Liturgy Training Publications, 1985. This book contains the major liturgical documents from Rome and the U.S. Bishops including: *Constitution on the Sacred Liturgy, General Instruction of the Roman Missal, Appendix to the General Instruction for the Diocese of the United States, Lectionary for Mass: Introduction, General Norms for the Liturgical Year and the Calendar, Directory for Masses with Children, Music in Catholic Worship, Liturgical Music Today,* and *Environment and Art in Catholic Worship.*

SELECTED PUBLISHERS

Augsburg-Fortress Publications, 426 S. Fifth St., P.O. Box 1209, Minneapolis, MN 55440.
Concordia Publishing House, 3558 S. Jefferson, St. Louis, MO 63118-3968.
GIA Publications, Inc., 7404 S. Mason Ave., Chicago, IL 60638.
Hope Publishing Company, 380 South Main Place, Carol Stream, IL 60188.
Liturgical Press, Collegeville, MN 56321.
Liturgy Training Publications, 1800 N. Hermitage Ave., Chicago, IL 60622-1101.
North American Liturgy Resources, 10802 N. 23rd. Ave., Phoenix, AZ 85029.
The Pastoral Press and NPM Publications, 225 Sheridan St., NW, Washington, DC 20011-1492.
Oregon Catholic Press, 5536 NE Hassalo, Portland, OR 97213.
World Library Publications, 3815 N. Willow Road, Schiller Park, IL 60176.

MUSIC

Alstott, Owen. *Respond and Acclaim*. Portland: Oregon Catholic Press, published annually.

Batastini, Robert, ed. *Exsultet (Easter Proclamation)*. Chicago: GIA, 1980.

Connolly, Michael. *We Live a Mystery*. Chicago: GIA, 1988. Recording, music collection, and octavos.

———"You Are My Inheritance, O Lord." Chicago: GIA, 1990.

Cooney, Rory and Gary Daigle. *Psalms for the Church Year, Vol. IV*. Chicago: GIA, 1991.

Gather. Chicago: GIA and Phoenix: North American Liturgy Resources, 1988.

Gelineau, Joseph. *The Grail/Gelineau Gradual*. Chicago: GIA, Volume 1, 1977; Volume 2, 1979. Contains the full set of Sunday Mass Responsorial Psalms, with antiphons as found in *Worship II*. Cantor Training Tapes (Chicago: GIA) is a complete cassette recording of these psalms.

Haas, David and Jeanne Cotter. *Psalms for the Church Year, Vol. III*. Chicago: GIA, 1989.

Haas, David and Marty Haugen. *Psalms for the Church Year*. Chicago: GIA, 1983.

Haugen, Marty. *Mass of Creation*. Chicago: GIA, 1984

———*Psalms for the Church Year, Vol. II*. Chicago: GIA, 1988.

Hymnal for Catholic Students. Chicago: GIA and Liturgy Training Publications, 1988.

International Comission on English in the Liturgy. *ICEL Lectionary Music*. Chicago: GIA, 1982.

———*ICEL Resource Collection*. Chicago: GIA, 1981.

Joncas, Michael. *Come to Me*. Chicago: GIA, 1989. A recording, music collection and octavos.

Proulx, Richard. *Eucharistic Prayer for Children II*. Chicago: GIA, 1982.

———*A Community Mass*. Chicago: GIA. 1970.

Lead Me, Guide Me: The African-American Catholic Hymnal. Chicago: GIA, 1987.

Psalms for All Seasons. Washington: NPM Publications, 1987.

Worship. 3rd ed. Chicago: GIA, 1986. Contains many of the Gelineau psalm settings. Separate guitar accompaniment edition available.

APPENDIX 3.
TRAINING EXERCISES
FOR CANTORS

BREATHING

1. Place the hands on the sides, above the waist. Take deep breaths and feel the expansion in the abdomen. When breathing properly for singing, the chest remains high and stable. The lungs fill with air, forcing natural expansion of the abdomen.

2. Take in a very deep breath. Blow it out slowly, sixteen slow beats, on the consonant *s*.

3. Pant, like a winded dog, making sure the air feels like it goes down below the belt line.

4. Practice breathing in these positions: both hands held high over the head, lying down face up, on all fours. These positions make it difficult for the chest to move, so that expansion must occur in the abdomen.

DICTION

5. Sing pure vowels: *ee, ay, ah, oh, oo*. Be sure that *ah* does not become *uh*. Exercises can be on a neutral syllable such as *nah, doh, tee, loo*. There are many more vowels than these in the English language, but singing these helps singers concentrate on listening and forming specific sounds correctly.

6. Pick any hymn and find all of the diphthongs. What are the two vowels of the diphthong? Practice holding the first, without any distortion, and adding the second at the very end. For fun, sing the hymn in a distorted *twang* style.

7. Examine the consonants in a hymn. Which ones are likely to be left off if the singer is not careful? Which consonants at the ends of words should be *elided*, or connected, with the following word? Which

should not, because the words will be unclear if they are? What are some of the voiced and unvoiced consonants? Which consonants need to be sung *before* the beat so that the word will sound *on time*? Where are there challenges with the consonant *r*? How should it be sung?

8. Practice interpreting the meaning of the words. Read a psalm aloud. Emphasize the words that are important to meaning. The *Workbook for Lectors and Gospel Readers* (Liturgy Training Publications) has the Sunday readings laid out to help readers learn this same skill. It will be helpful for cantors as a practice tool.

GESTURES

9. Practice gestures by mirroring the gestures of a good cantor. This can be one-on-one or with a group in a circle. The opening gesture is the most critical.

10. Direct an antiphon using the "Pitch/Rhythm" method.

VIDEO

11. Videotape cantors at practice or at Mass. A close look at themselves in the replay will tell cantors more than any teacher can. Watch for excess motion, like shuffling, and closed, uninviting facial expressions. Be careful as well of the opposite extremes. Stiff posture or excessively sweet expressions are just as problematic.

RHYTHM AND TEMPO

12. To increase rhythmic awareness and accuracy, sing a hymn on *tah* with one syllable on every subdivided beat. Example: "Jesus Christ Is Risen Today," sing *tah* on every eighth note.

13. Sing a hymn on counting numbers: *1 and 2 and 3 and 4 and.*

14. Point a text to sing to a psalm tone. Mark the groups of two and three. Sing the psalm and feel the lilting, vibrant rhythm this feeling of two and three provides.

15. In the church, sing a song, hymn, or acclamation with instrumentalists or the organist. Make sure that you are exactly together rhythmically. This is especially challenging when the cantor is in front

and the organ in back. Other cantors should listen in various places in the church, to help the cantor who is singing and to learn how their own voice might sound in different pews.

15. Sing a song or hymn with a tempo change, such as "Here I Am Lord." Make sure the cantor and instruments stay together.

THE MICROPHONE AND ANNOUNCEMENTS

16. Try out the microphone the cantor uses. Does it pick up sound from all sides? How close or far must the singer be? Are there problems with excess noise from air with consonants like *p* or *wh* ? How is that problem solved?

17. Practice making hymn announcements. Be clear and brief.

TEACHING

18. Teach a hymn or acclamation, with and without accompaniment. This will feel awkward at first, so do it a number of times before attempting it at Mass.

LITURGY

19. To test liturgical awareness, list everything that happens at Mass in order.

About the Author

Michael Connolly brings a wide range of Catholic liturgical experiences to *The Parish Cantor*. A native of Washington state, he earned a Bachelor's degree at the University of Washington and went on to complete a Master's and Doctorate in choral music at the University of Southern California. He observed the European church music scene as a Rotary International Scholar in Vienna, 1985-86. Connolly also plays guitar and piano. His compositions, including the collection *We Live a Mystery*, are written in both contemporary and classical styles. He has been a parish music director, teacher, and diocesan music specialist, and has presented workshops across the United States. Currently, Connolly is an Assistant Professor of Music and Director of Liturgical Music and the University of Portland, Portland, Oregon.